Words are powerful  nd they definitely help ur words prophesy ou g enough, and the cl d. In his book, *The F* n reminds us of just how powerful words can be, especially negative ones. Tim then gives concrete steps on how we can change our conversation, which in turn will change our future and ultimately change the world. Fast your way into a new future…through your words.

—Dr. Billy Wilson
President, Oral Roberts University

When I was asked to endorse this book, I knew that I could instantly say yes because I know the author and know he is a man of great character. Imagine my surprise to learn that he, of all people, had gotten to the place of negativity in life. Having gone through a forty-day fast from food in my own life, I well understand the value of fasting as a practice. As I have been reading this book, *The Forty-Day Word Fast*, I have come to the realization that I need this book! I have once again been reminded that I should not call myself anything less than my Father calls me—and that I should not devalue the life of another human being because my Father does not. The rich treasure trove you will find as you search your own heart as you read this book will be well worth it—for years to come!

—Dennis Jernigan
Worship leader, songwriter,
and internationally renowned
Christian recording artist

If life and death are in the power of the tongue, then *The Forty-Day Word Fast* by Tim Cameron will challenge you to a whole new perspective on life in Christ. Jesus calls us to a fasted lifestyle, and that includes our words. This book issues a clarion call to tame the tongue and to put into practice biblical yet simple keys that will change the course of your life forever.

—ROGER NIX
SENIOR PASTOR, BELIEVERS CHURCH
TULSA, OKLAHOMA

Jesus said it first, "But what comes out of the mouth proceeds from the heart, and this defiles a person." Paul said it later, "Do everything without complaining and arguing"; and, "Always be joyful. Never stop praying. Be thankful in all circumstances, for this is God's will for you who belong to Christ." Tim Cameron made a change in his life that was more than superficial. It was deep, painful, and profound. He got serious about being like Christ. His story cuts through all the excuses, and his method is clear and effective. What would the watching world say about us if we lived this way? I think they would say, "They look like they truly love one another. Maybe we should check this out."

—BILL HULL
AUTHOR, *JESUS CHRIST, DISCIPLEMAKER; CHRISTLIKE;*
THE DISCIPLE-MAKING PASTOR; AND
THE DISCIPLE-MAKING CHURCH

It's interesting that when I read Tim Cameron's book, God was getting serious with me about cynicism in my own life. One can become hindered by that "little fox" when one lives too long among Christians, as I have for the last four years, and not enough among the world's peoples where *exemplary* godly character is constantly required and always tested. This book was good for me, and it will be "healing medicine" for anyone with whom God is working such as He has been on me. Anytime God seeks to help us, there will be some "hurting" to do, and this book doesn't just "deaden the pain." It's practical, hopeful stuff here, but it doesn't let us off easy. I predict that most who read this book will emerge full of gratitude, which is Cameron's great antidote to the poison of those "little foxes."

—DR. ROBERT J. STAMPS
DEAN OF CHAPEL, ASBURY THEOLOGICAL SEMINARY

As I read this book by Tim Cameron, I was astonished at the practical wisdom, the deep honesty, and the biblical insight that came to me day by day. This book documents the ongoing work of the Holy Spirit in the life one man—who now offers to us the path to healing, wholeness, and holiness he has found. The invitation to live in the sanctifying grace of God that is contained in these pages, along with the process of daily spiritual reflection, comes with the assurance that "God did this for me, and I know God can do it for you."

—THOMAS R. ALBIN
DEAN OF THE UPPER ROOM MINISTRIES AND
ECUMENICAL RELATIONS
EXECUTIVE DIRECTOR OF THE UNITED CHRISTIAN
ASHRAMS OF NORTH AMERICA

Tim Cameron offers both deep spiritual insight and practical advice in *The Forty-Day Word Fast*. He transposes the spiritual discipline of fasting from food to fasting from certain words and attitudes that wound relationships and destroy the soul. The first part of the book offers a helpful theological understanding of how fasting from judgment, criticism, sarcasm, complaining, negative words, and gossip can free a person both to hear from others and pronounce over others the words of blessing that we all so desperately need. The second part of the book lays out a practical, forty-day plan to fast from these words and attitudes, and to make this spiritual discipline a habit of the heart in our everyday interactions with family, friends, and coworkers. It is a book that instructs and inspires us to live a more godly and full life, a resource that will benefit all who seek to follow Christ.

—Dr. Charles W. Pollard
President, John Brown University
Board Chair, Council for Christian
Colleges and Universities

The Forty-Day Word Fast

TIM CAMERON

CHARISMA
HOUSE

Most CHARISMA HOUSE BOOK GROUP products are available at special quantity discounts for bulk purchase for sales promotions, premiums, fund-raising, and educational needs. For details, write Charisma House Book Group, 600 Rinehart Road, Lake Mary, Florida 32746, or telephone (407) 333-0600.

THE FORTY-DAY WORD FAST by Tim Cameron
Published by Charisma House
Charisma Media/Charisma House Book Group
600 Rinehart Road
Lake Mary, Florida 32746
www.charismahouse.com

This book or parts thereof may not be reproduced in any form, stored in a retrieval system, or transmitted in any form by any means—electronic, mechanical, photocopy, recording, or otherwise—without prior written permission of the publisher, except as provided by United States of America copyright law.

Unless otherwise noted, all Scripture quotations are taken from the Modern English Version. Copyright © 2014 by Military Bible Association. Used by permission. All rights reserved

Scripture quotations marked ABPE are from the Original Aramaic New Testament in Plain English With Psalms and Proverbs, copyright © 2007; 8th edition copyright © 2013. All rights reserved. Used by permission.

Scripture quotations marked ISV are taken from the Holy Bible, International Standard Version®. Copyright © 1996-forever by The ISV Foundation. All rights reserved internationally. Used by permission.

Scripture quotations marked KJV are from the King James Version of the Bible.

Scripture quotations marked NAS are from the New American Standard Bible, copyright © 1960, 1962, 1963, 1968, 1971, 1972, 1973, 1975, 1977, 1995 by The Lockman Foundation. Used by permission. (www .Lockman.org)

Scripture quotations marked NIV are taken from the Holy Bible, New International Version®, NIV®. Copyright © 1973, 1978, 1984, 2011 by Biblica, Inc.™ Used by permission of Zondervan. All rights reserved worldwide. www.zondervan.com The "NIV" and "New International Version" are trademarks registered in the United States Patent and Trademark Office by Biblica, Inc.™

Scripture quotations marked NLT are from the Holy Bible, New Living Translation, copyright © 1996, 2004, 2007. Used by permission of Tyndale House Publishers, Inc., Wheaton, IL 60189. All rights reserved.

Copyright © 2015 by Tim Cameron
All rights reserved

Cover design by Vincent Pirozzi
Design Director: Justin Evans

Visit the author's website at
www.timcameronprayer.com.

Library of Congress Cataloging-in-Publication Data
Cameron, Tim.
  The forty-day word fast / by Tim Cameron. -- First
edition.
      pages cm
  ISBN 978-1-62998-221-2 (trade paper) -- ISBN 978-1-
62998-222-9 (e-book)
  1. Language and languages--Religious aspects--
Christianity. 2. Communication--Religious aspects--
Christianity. I. Title.
  BR115.L25C35 2015
  241'.672--dc23

                                    2015021129

While the author has made every effort to provide
accurate Internet addresses at the time of publication,
neither the publisher nor the author assumes any
responsibility for errors or for changes that occur after
publication.

19 20 21 22 23 — 13 12 11 10 9
Printed in the United States of America

I dedicate this book to my amazing family, grandkids, goddaughters, and friends: Annamae, who is so patient, and my loving children and their spouses who prayed me through the very dark times of illness these past years. Isaac, you taught me to play again. Cameron, you model for me every day the unrestrained joy of the Lord. Sam, you are full of the gentleness of Jesus. My goddaughters, you are trophies of God's sovereign majesty. My friends Ben, Hans, Paul, Kirk, Richard, Roger, Tom, and Bill, you have shown me what a faithful friend looks like. Lloyd, you believed in me and prayed daily through this journey.

CONTENTS

PREFACE

I COULD NEVER SEE myself as a writer. The idea of becoming a writer was once right up there with the possibility of being named head coach for the US Olympic soccer team. But here I am, writing this book, and there is a lesson in this. We don't see ourselves the way the Lord sees us. Too often when we look in the mirror, all we see are our past failures and sin. We see the broken relationships and lost opportunities. In short, we are chained to the past. However, when the Lord sees us, He doesn't see our sin. Our failures and transgressions have been thoroughly removed from His thoughts.

This book has been written because I am convinced the Lord wants us to quit living in the past. He wants His kingdom to come right now, in the middle of our everyday lives. You see, His kingdom isn't some ethereal, mystical land reserved for the ending of our lives. Though there is great mystery surrounding His kingdom, it is still quite clear what the kingdom of God looks like in our midst. It is knowing Christ intimately and being known by Him. And it is experiencing the indescribable joy of telling others about Him. It is having His righteousness, peace, and joy in our lives—"for the kingdom of God does not mean eating and drinking, but righteousness and peace and joy in the Holy Spirit" (Rom. 14:17).

The kingdom of God is not like the kingdom of this world. It operates in opposition to the world. The greatest in the kingdom is the least; to gain your life you must lose it; to receive you must give, whether that is forgiveness, mercy, kindness, or love.

The same truth of opposites is in operation with our words. If we are going to share with others the life of our Lord that leads to salvation, we must learn the language of the kingdom. There is no room in the kingdom for the negative words of this world. We can't lead others to Jesus if our language is sprinkled—much less saturated—with this world's words. The only place we can take people with those words is to the land of religion, not to a relationship with Christ.

You'll learn through this book that language of God's kingdom is quite different from that of this world. It is childlike, draws people into unity in Christ, and is full of grace, peace, and restoration. As we begin to speak this language, we will find the doors of the kingdom opened to us here and now.

It has been said that if you speak three languages, you are from the Far East; if you speak two languages, you are from Europe; if you speak one language, you are from the United States; and that it is next to impossible for a more mature person to learn a new language. But I have learned a new language, and it is a language any person can learn at any age.

Within these pages is my journey of learning this language of the kingdom, and I invite you to come along and make the journey your own. Make no mistake—it is an intensive journey, one that will ask for your commitment and attention. But it is also one that will teach you to speak the kind of language that reflects the simplicity and purity of the kingdom of God.

Introduction

FASTING FROM WORDS?

I HAVE ALWAYS STRUGGLED with being a positive person. Even though I was blessed with five healthy children, a wonderful and happy wife, opportunities to serve the Lord, a position as headmaster of a large and thriving Christian academy, professional esteem, and financial stability, still the glass was half empty. I felt a constant struggle to recognize and embrace the positives in my life.

Becoming a negative person crept up on me. I complained, was sarcastic, and delivered bad news to people regularly. One of the worst aspects was that I found a measure of joy in being the one to deliver bad news, sad news, negative news, or scandalous news to people. Also, I had refined a repertoire of self-effacing quips to subtly put myself down any time I was given a compliment. If someone told me he liked the suit I was wearing, I'd say something like, "Don't let it fool you." My operational mantra was, "When people try to turn over a new leaf, the same thing is on the other side."

My wife noticed it first, the way I had begun to complain about almost anything. From the weather to the guy driving in front of us, all I could see were opportunities to grumble. The truth is I resisted my wife's concern, and that was creating a real strain on our marriage. Soon the Lord began tugging at my heart to do something about this negative paradigm that had come home to roost in my life. Through self-examination I began to really hear the words that were flowing out of my mouth, and it wasn't pleasing to my ears. Negative attitudes and words were gushing out. I was shocked at the caustic, toxic verbal waste that my words represented. Many of the core beliefs I held about myself were being challenged. For instance, I prided myself on being able to keep a confidence, but incidents were surfacing where I transgressed. From judgments to gossip, I was being exposed to my own hypocrisy every time I opened my mouth.

It was difficult for me to own up to it, but I had become a complainer and a negative person. It was ruining my marriage and causing people to distance themselves from me.

Clearly the Lord had something better for me than pessimism and complaining. The quandary I faced was what to do about it. I tried positive self-help programs but simply could not get a breakthrough. Ordinarily such approaches toward life are encouraging and helpful. Most of us know and appreciate the power behind positive words and declarations. But I had strongholds that needed something more forceful and dramatic. In my desperate state I needed specific insights into what had to be weeded out of my life.

Late one night, in defeat and discouragement, the Lord guided me to these six words:

- Judgments
- Criticism

- Sarcasm
- Negativity
- Complaining
- Gossip

In a time of prayer and waiting on the Lord, I heard Him speak to me. He said, "It is time to fast the words you want to lay the axe to in your life. Some things only come out by fasting." I heard Him say, "Do a forty-day fast of these words."

I dove into God's final authority, His Word, for clarity and direction. I saw that the Scriptures make it profoundly clear that some things are accomplished only by fasting. From Christ's encounter with the devil in the wilderness to the disciples' inability to cast out a demon, we see that fasting coupled with prayer has greater power. Fasting is a spiritual discipline that carries the potential to energize God's power in our lives during dramatic times of need. We read in the Gospel of Mark, "When He had entered the house, His disciples asked Him privately, 'Why could we not cast it out?' He said to them, 'This kind cannot come out except by prayer and fasting'" (Mark 9:28–29).

And the Scriptures are replete with calls to fast. In one of the classic sections on fasting in Isaiah 58:6–9, Isaiah issues a challenge to choose the fast that can break the bonds and yokes to let the oppressed go free. Isaiah goes on to say that the Lord will hear and answer our cries if we remove the pointing of the finger and the speaking of wickedness. In fact, the word *fast* in the original Hebrew means "to cover [the mouth]."[1]

Our freedom from bondage is so often linked to the words that come out of our mouths from our hearts. I quickly saw these words of judgment, criticism, sarcasm, negativism, complaining, and gossip were to have no part in my life as a Christian.

When I embarked on a forty-day journey of fasting these words, a close friend walked alongside me. We both noticed the very first thing that happened: I started speaking less. I simply couldn't say much of what I was used to saying. Negative words weren't coming out of my mouth as often, and I found myself listening to people more. I was holding my tongue, and a huge volume of my daily verbiage was disappearing. I ended each day repenting of my transgressions and chronicling my transgressions in a journal that allowed me to be honest and concrete with myself.

Through this book I'm inviting you into a similar fast. The teaching chapters that follow in the first part of this book open your spiritual understanding to the negative words of this world and the consequences they produce in the lives of believers. In these chapters you will learn the syntax of the language of the kingdom. Read the chapters slowly and thoroughly. Make notes in the margins. Pray as you go, asking the Lord to prepare your heart for the forty-day word fast that follows in the second part of the book. During the actual forty-day word fast you will learn and practice the language of the kingdom. I encourage you to make a practice of reading the Scripture passage and devotional lesson for each day in the morning and then complete your journal entries in the evening.

I strongly believe this forty-day fast can change your life. You can find new freedom in relationships, discover inner peace, and free yourself from baggage you've carried around for years or a lifetime. You will build up your spiritual immune system and become less sensitive to potential offenses and criticism. You will stop being your own worst enemy, and your self-image will change. You'll stop sizing people up and judging them and will start to see people as the Lord sees them.

Consider other benefits to this. Can you imagine how much an employer would appreciate, praise, or promote an employee who never complained and wouldn't participate in gossip on the job? An employee like this is every boss's dream.

How monumentally would a teen stand out who didn't curse and instead spoke words of blessing to others, who didn't judge peers or teachers, who was positive and always looked on the possibility side of challenges, who wouldn't gossip about classmates or those in authority? A young person like this would be elevated to positions of honor and leadership. That person would stand head and shoulders above his peers in godliness and influence.

The decision is yours. Take the challenge. Walk into newness and freedom. The way others view you will change. More importantly, the way you view yourself will change. You will be freed from yourself.

Part One

An Orientation

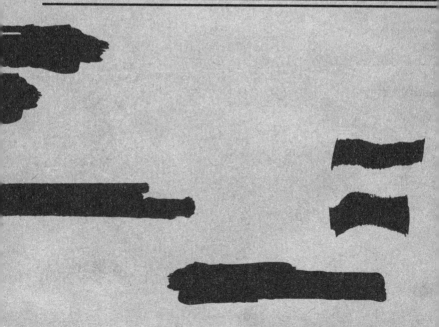

Chapter 1

THE POWER OF WORDS

A lie will go round the world while the
truth is putting its boots on.[1]
—CHARLES SPURGEON

MOST OF US understand the power of spoken words, at least to some degree, but it is likely uncharted territory for us to consider the power of *fasting* words, or not speaking specific words. How could this be powerful? Scripture tells us very pointedly, "We all err in many ways. But if any man does not err in word, he is a perfect man and able also to control the whole body" (James 3:2). There are some fiercely unruly members in our bodies, but God's Word says that if we tame our words, we can tame our body and mind. That's powerful!

The taming of these unruly members of our body—the tongue, the mind, the appetite—presents a formidable challenge. However, the truth of God's Word is, "I can do all things because of Christ who strengthens me" (Phil. 4:13). It is the truth that sets us free. And herein lies part of the paradigm shift that will take place in our lives as we fast words. We move from what is true to the truth, from the seen to the unseen, from the physical to the spiritual, from the negative to the hopeful. We will quit living in the past, allowing our failures, mistakes, and sin to paint our identity with hopelessness. We will move into God's intentions

1

and promises for us. We will see God's kingdom come to earth in our midst.

Can you visualize the impact on your life if you could bridle your thoughts and body? This is God's very intention for us, to destroy strongholds of poor self-image, negative speculations, and every thought that is contrary to who we are in Christ.

Life and death are in the power of the tongue. The words that come out of our mouths heal or hurt. They bring reconciliation or division. By our words men are called into their destiny and the life of the Lord is shared with others. By words dreams are shattered.

You see, Satan is always out to destroy the essential purposes of God. Christ's vision for us as believers is that we might be one as He and the Father are one. Christ knew our great love for one another would draw unbelievers into the kingdom as they witnessed something their souls yearned for but could not find in the world: unconditional acceptance and love. Satan uses these other kinds of words that come out of our mouths—judgments, criticism, sarcasm, negativity, complaining, and gossip—to keep this purpose of God at bay.

Words of blessing have a remarkable impact. Gentle words of blessing soothe the inner man. They are like cherry limeade with crushed ice on a sweltering summer's day, refreshing the body and emotions. Words of encouragement bolster the will and activate hope in our lives. Each one of us yearns for motivating words of praise that infuse our self-worth. They stimulate our desire to actualize the unique potential God has placed in each one of us. Sunny, cheery words are protein to the spirit of a child, shaping the course of his or her life at such a tender age and having eternal impact.

Positive words are verbal nutrients that hydrate the entire being; when lacking, God's purposes are left dormant. Negative words produce verbal toxins that poison the soul. In the wake of negative, critical words, a person's confidence is destroyed and God's possibilities are crushed. Yes, spoken words have the power of life and death.

As Christians we are commissioned to be ambassadors of life to others, to speak blessing not curses. Words that are judgmental, critical, sarcastic, negative, complaining, or soaked with gossip cast a dark cloud on everyone who comes in contact with them. These words should have no part of us. Paul teaches us directly, "Let no unwholesome word proceed out of your mouth, but only that which is good for building up, that it may give grace to the listeners" (Eph. 4:29).

A CULTURE OF POLLUTION

One of the significant challenges we face is the toxic verbal culture in which we live. Perhaps the greatest behavioral principle of life is that people repeat the behavior they see others perform. We are influenced and impacted by what is happening around us. Today's culture is out of control and has no moral compass or protective boundaries around it when it comes to the spoken word. Just about anything is fair game, and no one is off-limits.

The "F-bomb" is common to everyday language and rampant in all venues of the entertainment industry. Just take in the evening news, go to a movie, listen to the popular talk show hosts on the radio, or lend an ear to unsuspecting teens as they are engaged in uninhibited dialogue. What you will hear on the evening news are vulgar descriptions of unimaginable acts, spoken live on television for anyone to hear. Even going for a family movie night exposes one to raunchy, foul-mouthed previews of upcoming films. Turn on the radio, and you'll hear the talk show hosts demean, criticize, and mock everyone and anyone; from the president of the United States to the pope, no one is safe from their constant diatribes immersed in four-letter words and sprinkled with uninhibited sexual overtones.

The vernacular of most young people today is nothing short of shameful. For fifteen years I was a public school principal at the middle school and high school levels. Honestly, it would be challenging for me to articulate the nonstop stream of vulgarity and profanity I heard day in and day out.

The issue at hand, however, is not the mouth but the heart. Jesus preached on this in many places of Scripture, such as in Mark 7:20–23, where He said, "What comes out of a man is what defiles a man. For from within, out of the heart of men, proceed evil thoughts, adultery, fornication, murder, theft, covetousness, wickedness, deceit, licentiousness, an evil eye, blasphemy, pride and foolishness. All these evil things come from within and defile a man."

Yes, the heart is the issue. The Lord is calling for hearts to be changed, made sweet, tender, soft, and able to receive the things of His Spirit. What is in the well comes up in the bucket. The words that condemn us—judgments, criticism, sarcasm, negativity, complaining, and gossip—come from deep within a heart that needs purification from the Creator.

My experience concurs with the psychological and educational research that claims negative, damaging words have far greater impact than positive words.[2] I have witnessed it over and over again in teachers and coaches who bark berating words that attack a child's self-image. The teacher gets his or her needs met at the expense of the student. Their impact is long lasting—they sour children on education, and their negative effect destroys the efforts of so many other skilled, kind professionals. It is as if no matter how many positive mentors a student has at school, one negative, insensitive, caustic adult can spoil the whole environment for that young person.

Systematic behavior management of children is a major domain of discussion and research in education today. Nearly all such curriculums on behavior management hold the common belief that to correct young people or to give them instructional feedback that they do not see as positive requires you to first deposit many positive seeds of encouragement to out-weigh the one word perceived as corrective or nega-tive. Most protagonists of this philosophy identify the needed ratio of at least three positive reinforcements to one corrective or perceived negative response.

Simply put, we underestimate the greater power of negative words. But Scripture is quite clear about the power of these words, teaching us they are devas-tating to our spirit. Proverbs 15:4 tells us, "A wholesome tongue is a tree of life, but perverseness in it crushes the spirit." The Scriptures also tells us to flee from the pres-ence of people who emit destructive words of gossip and judgments: "He who goes about as a talebearer reveals secrets; therefore do not meddle with him who flatters with his lips" (Prov. 20:19). And let's be honest: none of us enjoy being around a person whose speech is loaded with complaining and negativity.

Ridding our lives of these destructive words requires dramatic action and dogged persistence. Self-help authors have long said it takes at least twenty-one days of changed behavior to break the cycle of a bad habit.[3] The Lord's instruction in this and other matters always goes deeper and is more thorough. He's not looking for a quick or temporary fix. He's looking for eradication. He calls for a forty-day fast to break the chains.

If you've ever fasted, you've probably experienced the dynamic power it can release in your life to become free from sin, to pray for God's blessing on others, and to establish intimacy with the Lord. This same power can be released in your life by fasting negative words. You can break the bonds and yokes in your life that words of judgment, criticism, sarcasm, negativity, complaining, and gossip create. This is the fast Isaiah refers to that I mentioned earlier, a fast that removes the pointing of the finger and the speaking of wickedness:

> Is not this the kind of fasting I have chosen: to loose the chains of injustice and untie the cords of yoke, to set the oppressed free and break every yoke?
>
> —ISAIAH 58:6, NIV

Verse 9 gives us this promise:

> Then you will call, and the LORD will answer; you will cry for help, and he will say: Here am I. If you do away with the yoke of oppression, with the pointing finger and malicious talk...
>
> —NIV

In this process we are out for a fast that doesn't just give a reprieve from these damaging words but a permanent removal of them. Is it possible? All things are possible to him who believes.

We are spiritual and physical beings. What takes place in us physically impacts our soul. As we bring these negative words in our life under the control of the Holy Spirit, a dramatic transaction will take place in our mind, emotions, and will. Our mind will become clear and uncluttered. Our emotions will become more stable. And there will be a new impetus in our will to desire the precepts and life of Christ.

YOUR SPIRITUAL IMMUNE SYSTEM

A recent research endeavor has broken new ground in understanding the effects of fasting on us physically. This scientific research has discovered that fasting two to four days flips a renewal switch in our stem cells and prompts cell-based regeneration of new white blood cells in the body's defense system.[4]

I believe this discovery has monumental spiritual ramifications for us regarding the fasting of words. This is what the Lord has revealed to me: When we bring the words that come out of our mouths under the control of the Holy Spirit through the fasting of words, our spiritual immune system is regenerated and strengthened. If we suffer from long-standing strongholds with our negative words or are damaged in our souls as a result of the verbal attacks of other people, our fasting of words has an even greater exponential effect in a positive manner. The multiplied, pressed-down, and shaken-over judgments we would have experienced from others as by-product of our judgments on them disappear. Our spiritual immune system is energized as we fast these damaging words. Our spirit man builds up immunity to the verbal attacks others send our way. Healing takes place in our soul from the caustic words of parents who made mistakes, friends who gossiped about us, and coworkers who judged us for whatever reason they had. These normally damaging words lose their impact on us. We become offense-proof.

Jesus tells us in Matthew 18:7 that offenses are going

to come. Can you see yourself offense-proof from the negative words of others? Can you see yourself insulated from the constant flow of judgments, criticism, sarcasm, negativity, complaining, and gossip that permeates our world? Imagine not giving any weight to the judgments or criticism of others. Someone makes an insensitive comment about how you look tired and worn out, and it has no impact on you because your spiritual immune system is in full force.

As powerful as negative words are, the fasting of such words has a reciprocal impact that is mightier. The great power negative words have over positive words begins to work in reverse. Every time we hold our tongue and don't make those negative comments, others consider us wise for our silence. Every time we put a halt to that critical thought we were about to utter, we bring our minds and body under control. Every time we don't speak that negative word, we distance ourselves from our past failures. Every time we don't complain, we reinforce gratefulness in our lives. Every time we don't pass gossip on to others, we purify our lives so other people have less to gossip to others about us.

Words have great power. However, bringing these words of judgment, criticism, sarcasm, negativity, complaining, and gossip under the governance of the Holy Spirit through the fasting of them has a powerful serendipitous effect. The words we *do* speak are purified. Selfish motives we're not aware of disappear. Our words begin to speak into the unseen, into the spiritual realm. We begin to speak with the words of a disciple. We hear God's words spoken through our tongue, and our words begin to sustain others:

> The Lord GOD has given me the tongue of the learned, that I may know how to sustain him who is weary with a word; He awakens me morning by morning; He awakens my ear to listen as the learned.
>
> —ISAIAH 50:4

Submit your life and words to this forty days of fasting words, and you can be graced with the tongue of a disciple.

Chapter 2

RENDER NOT JUDGMENT

To judge: to make an evaluation as to the value,
quality, or capability of others, or one who thinks
he or she knows why others do what they do.

WHEN WE SEE people respond a particular way and draw a conclusion about why they acted as they did, we are judging. What a penetrating and sobering thought—to presume we have the discernment, personal knowledge, or position in life to determine another person's quality, their capability, or why they did what they did. What audacity. There is one judge, and He is altogether righteous and able to see into the hearts of men or women. We are not that judge; Christ is. This understanding is crucial to comprehend the issue of judging.

James 4:11 exhorts us:

> Brothers and sisters, do not slander one another. Anyone who speaks against a brother or sister or judges them speaks against the law and judges it. When you judge the law, you are not keeping it, but sitting in judgment on it.
>
> —NIV

The critical issue to understand is that we don't know what is in the heart of man; only God knows that. Jeremiah 17:9–10 says, "The heart is more deceitful than all things and desperately wicked; who can

11

understand it? I, the Lord, search the heart, I test the mind, even to give to every man according to his ways, and according to the fruit of his deeds." It doesn't take the wisest man on the face of the earth to comprehend that God is the only one who understands, searches, and tests the heart of man. King Solomon was the wisest man on the face of the earth, and he articulated a clear grasp of this issue when he called out to God, "Then hear in heaven Your dwelling place, and forgive, and act, and render to everyone according to all his ways, whose hearts You know—for only You know the hearts of the sons of men" (1 Kings 8:39).

When you judge others, you are in deception. The problem with deception is, you don't realize you're being deceived. You see and hear wrongly. You think the sky is red, but everyone around you knows the sky is blue. You would swear on your life the sky is red; it isn't. Could there be a minute possibility, an outside chance existing in your wildest imagination, that there may be a tiny prospect you are wrong? When you are in deception, you answer that question with a vehement *no*. You need new spiritual tools to help you see and hear. You need your spiritual eyes and ears opened.

When we think we know a person's motivation for saying or doing something, we are playing God. Of the multitude of circumstances in life we can find ourselves in, this is the one not to be found in: playing God in people's lives and judging them.

THE ECONOMY OF JUDGMENT

There are a small number of crucial issues in the Christian life foundational to walking in peace and fruitfulness before the Lord and with people, and the issues include forgiveness, humility, and judging. These issues affect almost every area of our life: friendships, marriage, children, work, and ministry. Understanding these key issues is the difference between being a fruitful disciple of Jesus or a defeated spectator of the Christian faith. We simply can't afford to get these issues wrong; the emotional cost is too high.

Judging others creates great emotional turmoil and pain in our lives, far beyond what we understand in the natural realm. Why is it such a central issue in life? Simply put, it encapsulates the fullness of Jesus's teachings in Luke 6:27–38 that we receive back more than we give to others, good and bad. Christ tells us in this passage:

> But I say to you who hear, love your enemies, do good to those who hate you, bless those who curse you, and pray for those who spitefully use you. To him who strikes you on the one cheek, offer also the other. And from him who takes away your cloak, do not withhold your tunic as well. Give to everyone who asks of you. And of him who takes away your goods, do not ask for them back. Do unto others as you would have others do unto you.
>
> —LUKE 6:27–31

Pretty radical teaching, huh? It gets more extreme! He continues:

> Love your enemies, and do good, and lend, hoping for nothing in return. Then your reward will be great, and you will be the sons of the Highest. For He is kind to the unthankful and the evil. Be therefore merciful, even as your Father is merciful.
>
> —LUKE 6:35–36

These radical teachings of Jesus provoke us to ask the question, Could Jesus have really meant what He said? The answer is yes, He did!

These teachings scandalize our natural thought process. They are what I call *spiritual sympathies*. We may be sympathetic with the teachings, but we can only fully understand and appreciate them through a spiritual paradigm of life. As 1 Corinthians 2:14 teaches, "The person without the Spirit does not accept the things that come from the Spirit of God but considers them foolishness, and cannot understand them because they are discerned only through the Spirit" (NIV).

Jesus goes on to finish His teaching in Luke with reverse parallels that add simplicity and clarity to His teaching:

> Judge not, and you shall not be judged. Condemn not, and you will not be condemned. Forgive, and you shall be forgiven.
>
> —LUKE 6:37

Verse 38 is the key verse in understanding the unimaginable repercussions of judging:

> Give, and it will be given to you: Good measure, pressed down, shaken together, and running over will men give unto you. For with the measure you use, it will be measured unto you.

We hear this verse applied to financial matters regularly, and that makes some sense. However, what Christ is really expressing here is that what I extend to others—loving, blessing, mercy, forgiveness, a refrain from judgment and condemnation—is what I will get back from others, only in greater abundance. This verse is not about God judging me if I judge other people. Jesus is saying that if I judge people, these other people will judge me back, only with greater measure and running over.

This scripture is about the exchanges we have with other people—our personal interactions. It's about the investment we make in others bearing greater return in our lives as positive and negative investments. When we show mercy, we receive more mercy back. When we condemn, we will receive greater condemnation back. When we forgive others, they will extend greater mercy and forgiveness to us. When we judge others, we will be judged much more harshly. Simply put, when we judge others, we receive back judgments beyond what we can comprehend.

How important is it that we get this teaching of Christ right? If your goal is to lead a peaceful and fruitful life, it is paramount that you thoroughly understand this teaching. Of all the ends in life that we crave and long after, the realization of peace in our family, relationships, work, and community of fellowships and churches ranks near the pinnacle. Ridding our lives of judgmental words is a key to finding this peace.

ARE YOU SURE YOU KNOW?

What does it really mean to judge someone? Let's return to the definition offered at the beginning of this chapter: *making evaluation as to the value, quality, or capability of others or thinking we know why others do what they do.*

Perhaps it's as easy to explain what judging is by addressing what it's not. Watching life take place around you and observing someone's actions is not judging. When you look at actions, you see results or fruit.

These are the two ways we actually judge people: when you see someone's actions and you make an estimate as to the value, quality, or capability of that person, or when you think you know why he did what he did. You think you know his motivation.

How do we judge others? Let's look at the following example.

Many of us have experienced this scenario. The pastor races by us on his way to do something at church. He doesn't stop to pay particular attention to us. He doesn't catch a hello or greeting sent to him as he whizzes by. What is your immediate response? Do you respond graciously, realizing the pastor has a lot on his plate that morning, or do you respond with a judgment that draws a conclusion about how insensitive and unfriendly he is? Do you compound it further with gossip by mentioning to someone else how unfriendly your pastor was today?

In this example we have the embodiment of one of the primary ways we judge others. In that instant we think we have the perceptive ability to look into a person's heart and know why he acted a particular way—we judge. What pride and arrogance.

I've been on the other end of this and know how off-base judgments can be. Some years ago I became the high school principal at a large school. One of the benefits of being the principal was having a nice office and my own private bathroom. I took my home-schooled daughter with me to the school to start her high school career.

It is tough enough to be the new kid on the block in high school, but to be the principal's daughter is exponentially tenuous. Lizzy immediately took over my bathroom as her makeup sanctuary because she had to rise early to ride with me every morning to school and I arrived very early. As Lizzy began to develop a few new relationships, a couple of the girls she befriended would come in the back door to my office to be with her in the bathroom doing their makeup in the morning. It was a time of constant giggling and squealing. When the first hour bell rang, they raced out.

Now if you have ever visited the public restroom for students in high school, you understand it isn't the most edifying place to hang out, win friends, and influence people. It was easy for me to tolerate the minor inconvenience of having my daughter and her friends in my office bathroom in the morning to facilitate my delightful daughter's easing into a new environment and relationships.

But it wasn't long before I began to catch drifts of rumors, criticism, and gossip from some of my staff about high school girls hanging out in the principal's office. It appeared my motives and intentions were being judged and scrutinized. I chose to not try to squelch the criticism and rumors, and in a few short months Lizzy had a new set of friends and was meeting them at their lockers in the morning, going to lunch, and, yes, entering that forbidden zone of the girls' restroom.

The chatter died down with the staff, and they found I was just a normal guy, not someone with hidden motives or a severe lack of discretion. But the truth is, I was being judged. Many faculty members were being insensitive and judgmental by not understanding my motives and the challenges my daughter faced as the principal's kid.

Have you ever watched someone fidget in a meeting and thought to yourself he must be bored and can't wait to get out of there? If you did, you made a judgment about the person's state of mind. You probably also took it to the extreme of concluding the person was insensitive and disrespectful. That's the problem with judging—it's like piling on in football, one judgment drawing another until we have buried the person we are judging under an avalanche of negative judgments.

Trust me, I struggle with this too. In the midst of my second time around on the forty-day word fast—yes, I completed it twice; my track record confirms I am a little hardheaded!—I began to see a problematic addiction that had developed in my life. I was unable to set my phone down for long periods of time. I never thought I would make the transition from the Bible hard copy to the Bible app, but there I was in church with my Bible app open on my smartphone and, oops, checking my e-mail now and then. I brought the addiction before the Lord in one of my devotional times on the forty-day word fast and asked Him to speak to my heart what was taking place.

Immediately the scene popped into my mind of the several judgments I had leveed on a person I supervised in the past. This person's inability to put down his smartphone irritated me in staff meetings and other public gatherings. Instead of appealing to him or encouraging him toward a healthy management of this new technology, I judged him harshly. I repented of that judgment on that day and have found the freedom and strength to put down the phone too.

There is a distinct clue when someone is judging another person or when we are in self-deception about our own intentions. You just have to listen to the words being used that profess to know the intensions of someone else's heart. We deceive ourselves and judge others with these kinds of statements:

- "I know why that person did what she did."
- "The person is really greedy."
- "I didn't mean those words that way; that isn't in my heart."
- "She sure is stuck on herself."
- "You know I would never hurt anyone on purpose."

The Scriptures are so consistent and revealing in this area of believing we know another person's motivations (or even our own!). God is the one who knows what is in our hearts—the motivations, desires, addictions, lusts, good, and bad. Psalm 44:21 asks, "Would not God search this out? For He knows the secrets of the heart." Again Acts 15:8 confirms, "God, who knows the heart, approved of them, giving them the Holy Spirit just as He did to us." In the end it is only God who truly knows the heart and intention of a person. We must be very careful in this matter of making judgments.

WHOM CAN WE BLAME?

Before Adam fell, he didn't walk around the garden making judgments about everything he observed. He didn't say, "Those berries are good, but Lord, I wish You had made them another color," or, "That Eve, I think her ears stick out too much." No, Adam didn't judge God's creation. Everything was good to Adam because he hadn't partaken of the tree of the knowledge of good and evil. He didn't judge. If he needed to know something, guess whom he asked? The Lord.

The reason God through the Holy Spirit wants to remove judgments from our hearts and from our mouths is because of the chains judgments create on our life. Before Adam fell, he was in perfect relationship with all of God's creation; everything was good. When he and Eve gained the understanding of good and evil from the tree in the middle of the garden, they also got something they didn't bargain for: fear. Fear welled inside them immediately when they sinned. Watch for it in Genesis 3:8: "Then they heard the sound of the LORD God walking in the garden in the cool of the day, and the man and his wife hid themselves from the presence of the LORD God among the trees of the garden."

Fear is the worst motivation for making decisions. My wife once spoke the truth to me that in the most challenging times of my spiritual life, I made decisions from two motivations: fear or finances. My financial indecision, bad decisions, and nondecisions were all a reflection of fear, making the judgment that God couldn't be trusted.

I believe many of the difficult experiences in my life have been the by-product of not recognizing and assuming responsibility for my actions. It is tantalizingly easy to look at a difficulty and scan the horizon for someone to blame. And if there isn't someone we can ascribe blame to, well, there is always the devil. In reality, most of our challenges come from two sources:

1. **We have made poor decisions and are experiencing the consequences.** Our loving heavenly Father is allowing us to be disciplined through these consequences to show us we belong to Him and He loves us. Most of us find it tough to accept this answer because it means we have no one to blame but ourselves.

2. **God is testing us.** Wait a minute. God is testing us? Yes. You see, He wants to be able to trust us. To ensure He can trust us, He tests us. He wants the crucial issues of our life—like this one, not judging—to be so embedded in our spirits that they become our testimony and the platform from which we share and minister to others. First Thessalonians 2:4 testifies to this, saying, "But as we were allowed by God to be entrusted with the gospel, even so we speak, not to please men, but God, who examines our hearts."

We often act like little children when it comes to assuming responsibility for our actions. The chocolate can be dripping down our face, but we deny eating it. We wiggle, squirm, and blame anyone except ourselves. There is no need for the enemy to deceive us; we are in self-deception. We are like this little guy. The seven-year-old boy beckoned me over to him as I was walking through the main office. He was sitting on the elementary principal's "time-out" chair waiting for his mom to arrive for a conference. When I came up to him, he motioned for me to come closer. Then he whispered to me, "I didn't really do it." As I found out later, he really did do it.

Being real with ourselves about areas of needed growth, mistakes, or just plain sin is the foundation for being responsible for our life in Christ. Understanding that there are consequences for errors and that because the Lord loves us He disciplines us will bring great freedom—the freedom to take conscious control of how we respond to all the circumstances of life.

How Not to Judge

> So from now on we regard no one from a worldly point of view. Though we once regarded Christ in this way, we do so no longer. Therefore, if anyone is in Christ, the new creation has come: The old has gone, the new is here!
>
> —2 Corinthians 5:16–17, niv

Judging others has become second nature to most of us. It is such a part of us it goes unnoticed and runs rampant throughout our day and lives. But where does it come from?

Words and thoughts of judgment are a function of the sin nature and expose our need for a heart change. Also, we judge others because we are influenced by the negative world we live in. So, how do we stop these judgments we are warned about by Jesus in Matthew 7:1–3?

First, we must stop thinking we can know the

intentions of a person's heart—why he says what he says or does what he does. Only God knows the heart.

Another important key is to quit drawing conclusions about people based on their outward actions. Try simply being an observer instead of looking at a person's actions and thinking he or she is bad, insincere, or rude. A person may have done a bad or hurtful thing, but that doesn't make him "bad." Drawing these kind of conclusions about people is responding to them after a worldly point of view. It is judging. Despite the person's actions, he is who God says he is, not what the world says.

If we don't judge others, then what are we supposed to do? Every day we are faced with situations where we have to make decisions or draw conclusions. It is part of life. Do I want to develop a friendship with him? Is she trustworthy enough for me to share a personal prayer request with her? Should I let my children play with the neighbor's children?

Here's what I believe we should do. First, we must live in the Spirit. This means we choose daily to rely on the Holy Spirit to guide our thoughts, words, and actions. If we do this, the Holy Spirit will give us the discernment we need to make decisions. The Bible says, "For those who live according to the flesh set their minds on the things of the flesh, but those who live according to the Spirit, the things of the Spirit. To be carnally minded is death, but to be spiritually minded is life and peace" (Rom. 8:5–6). When we walk in the Spirit, our minds are focused on the things of God, not the things of the world, so we will not judge after the flesh or the way of the world.

Secondly, we should observe the fruit of someone's life. The Bible says, "The fruit of the Spirit is love, joy, peace, patience, gentleness, goodness, faith, meekness, and self-control; against such there is no law" (Gal. 5:22–23). We must ask ourselves if the fruit of that person's life and actions is love, peace, joy, patience, kindness, goodness, faithfulness, gentleness, and self-control. Through the discernment of the Holy Spirit and by observing a person's fruit, we can decide if we want to develop a friendship with someone or let our children be involved with another family. This is the way we should make our everyday life decisions.

We gain freedom from judging others when we look to the Word of God and decide to understand others by the Spirit and by their fruit. We ask *what* instead of *why*. We don't try to look into someone's heart; we just look at their fruit. Matthew 7:16 says, "You will know them by their fruit. Do men gather grapes from thorns, or figs from thistles?"

The result of freeing ourselves from speaking damaging words of judgment is that we no longer receive the pressed-down, multiplied-back judgments of others, and we find new freedom to stop judging the person to whom our judgments are most damaging: ourselves. As we stop judging others, we discontinue looking to others for our self-worth. We no longer justify our own actions. We free ourselves from our judgments of ourselves and begin to walk as who we really are, new creations in Christ. His kingdom comes to earth in our midst, our minds are renewed, and we begin to think differently. We experience the reality of Romans 12:2: "Do not be conformed to this world, but be transformed by the renewing of your mind, that you may prove what is the good and acceptable and perfect will of God." Praise God.

Chapter 3

THE SARCASTIC WOUNDER
AND THE CRITIC

*Sarcasm: a remark made usually to hurt
someone's feelings or show scorn.*

THE WORD *SARCASM* is derived from the Greek verb *sarkazein*. It literally means "to tear flesh like a dog." Could there be a clearer, viler picture of sarcasm?[1]

Sarcasm has been labeled the lowest form of humor. Its prominence in social interaction and communication today demonstrates the depths to which we have fallen in our humor, and it is unfortunately alive and well in Christian circles too. Those who employ sarcasm argue that it's a higher form of humor because it requires intellectual prowess, quick wit, and the ability to extract the minutest point of weakness in a person or conversation. However, the use of sarcasm reveals how we use our mental capacity in a negative manner. The heart of sarcasm is mental judgments—drawing conclusions about what someone else is thinking and getting inside their head. This line of thinking exposes the base worldliness of sarcasm as a form of humor, worldly to the core.

THE MENTAL JOUST

Contemporary culture glorifies sarcasm as the pinnacle of humor. The more sarcastic you are, the more clever you're understood to be in your quips and comebacks. For some, sarcasm has become a ritual. The one-upmanship in sarcastic bantering resembles two fencers thrusting swords and wounding each other with emotional, cutting jabs until one submits or succumbs.

Brutal, sarcastic humor dominates the entertainment industry, from movies to television, and it influences our culture markedly. Look at the most popular comedians, talk show hosts, and highest-rated comedies on television, and you will see people vastly skilled in the art of raunchy, biting sarcasm. Their influence has colored our daily interactions with some of the following popular quips:

- "If I promise to miss you, will you go away?"
- "He's not the sharpest tool in the shed."
- "The same people who said the earth was flat wrote the Bible."
- "Did you forget to take your medication today?"

Sadly some of the sharpest, most mean-spirited sarcasm takes place in the political realm—or for that matter, toward anyone in authority—and pastors are not excluded. It is as though our leaders can't be human today. The simplest error in pronouncing a name or remembering a detail results in their being the butt of hypersarcastic jokes by every comedian for the next week.

Many Christians have lost their way on the issue of respect for our authorities, having fallen in line with the world in its sarcasm, disrespect, and lack of honor for those whom God has placed over us. What should be our response to these placed by God over us? First Timothy 2:1–2 exhorts us, "Therefore I exhort first of all that you make supplications, prayers, intercessions, and thanksgivings for everyone, for kings and for all who are in authority, that we may lead a quiet and peaceful life in all godliness and honesty."

As if it couldn't get worse, our children emulate the sarcastic exchanges that have come to be the most popular vehicle for humor. The more gross and vulgar the sarcasm of the world, the more wildly it is applauded and imitated by many young people. Sarcastic bantering has become a staple with our teens. A young person skilled in sarcastic jokes about "yo mama" and obesity can rise to the top in popularity. I heard comments like this and many more when I visited classrooms as a school principal. A helpful student would do something for a teacher, and someone in the back of the class would remark (in a tone the teacher couldn't hear), "Well, aren't you the teacher's little helper?" Of course, what followed was laughter by everyone within hearing distance of these sarcastic words.

Is This Normal?

Because sarcasm is so widely accepted, many have become desensitized to its rudeness and offense. It is accepted as normal; it's just another form of humor. Well, it's not just another form of humor, and it brings dishonor to the name of Christ for those who follow Him to use it. We are called to edify, not tear down.

We are commissioned to share the promises of God with His children, not destroy their self-image. Our charge is to be in the world, not of the world, to not blindly follow the practices of the world just to be accepted or look humorous.

I had a teacher at a Christian school who said *scarcasm* instead of *sarcasm*. She saw and understood the emotional wounding that sarcasm produces.

If sarcasm is so wounding, why is it employed by so many? I believe Christians who use sarcasm do not understand who they are in Christ. They have a poor self-image or live with a victim mentality and get their need for approval met by demeaning others. If we walked in the fullness of who we are in Christ, there would be a freedom in our lives that would obliterate the need to put others down and promote ourselves. Those who are seated with Christ in heavenly places are able to traverse the kingdom of heaven here on earth.

Suffice it to say, sarcastic criticism and bantering about a brother or sister in the Lord must be strongly discouraged in order for our fellowships and churches to mature and be all that Christ intended them to be as lights in the world.

WHY DO PEOPLE USE SARCASM?

- **Low self-esteem: Low self-esteem makes some people use any tool at hand to win acceptance and be revered by others.**

- Lack of self-confidence: A person with low self-confidence is often negative. They send negative messages everywhere in a desperate attempt to ascend over others.

- The influence of the world: Becoming "worldly" is deceptive and subtle. It leads people to just fall in line with what everyone is doing.

- Anger: Angry people get their needs met at the expense of others.

- Pain: Hurting others is a way of projecting blame on others for our own pain.

THE CRITIC'S CURSE

Criticism: the act of expressing disapproval and of noting the problems or faults of a person or thing; the act of criticizing someone or something; a remark or comment that expresses disapproval of someone or something.[2]

Who would purposefully choose to be a critical person? It means you can never relax and enjoy anything. You're always on the lookout to find fault in whatever is happening around you at any given moment. You look for the worst and miss the best. What's more, it makes you and everyone around you miserable. No one likes to be around a faultfinder, a person who is critical about everything.

The critic always responds the same way when presented with any opportunity, problem, challenge, or new relationship. He or she responds with a quick evaluation and synopsis of what can go wrong. It is the second nature of a critic to criticize; it comes as effortlessly as breathing. The critic's immediate response leaves others gasping and shaking their heads. Speaking of which, I will never forget an incident when all of my managers were gathered for a crucial presentation given by a seasoned consulting group. Their credentials and experience were impressive. They had proven success in addressing the serious issues we were facing. But following their recommendations, one of my key people responded with his normal critical assessment: "It will not work here."

How does one become a critical person? My personal example is germane here. I could not withstand the pressures of life. As a young man I struggled with the sins all young men encounter, and I did not have a spiritual foundation and identity in Christ to withstand temptations. The legalism of the religious system I was raised in didn't practice or understand restoration; therefore, I was reticent to confess my sin and seek help. Then there were the traumas of life, and I had a boatload.

For many of us, difficult life experiences as a child or young adult can easily cast us in the role of victim. We feel sorry for ourselves, pity ourselves, and begin the descent into the only role where we can get ahead of others: the critic. The message I perceived from my religious upbringing was "Work a little harder at being a Christian, sacrifice more, and serve more." Working harder was the answer to every problem, spiritual and physical. Sound familiar? The Pharisees were the pen-ultimate critics, and they labored more than anyone else at being religious, all for naught. Instead, they ended up being the ones Jesus railed against (though He used reason, not criticism).

THE SECRET CRITIC

Criticism poses a huge obstacle to the development of authentic spiritual community, and it is the gravest of dangers in the church. Our fellowship as Christians must be carefully cultivated, like a fledgling plant or a sapling. Once established, this fellowship can be very thick-skinned and can withstand almost any direct attack, but it is vulnerable to pressures from within.

The greatest danger to this fellowship? Criticism. And the most insidious danger to fellowship is *secret* criticism—criticism hidden in the recesses of the heart and not spoken.

Our fellowship with one another is based on trust. Criticism, even secret criticism, destroys that trust. Because we are spiritual beings and the ways of the Spirit operate in the unseen, secret criticism is every bit destructive as openly critical words, if not more so. Secret criticism hidden in the heart and never voiced makes us reticent to open up to each other. But our spirits are aware of it even if we don't understand what is transpiring in the natural. When there is secret criti-cism of the heart in operation in our Christian fel-lowship, it hinders honesty and authenticity. We don't know what's wrong, but something just doesn't feel right. Ever have those feelings?

There is only one appropriate response for coming to the recognition that you are holding any criticism in your heart toward another Christian, spoken or unspoken. That response is to confess the criticism for what it is: sin. Confessing my sin of criticism and judgment to another person is both humbling and freeing.

The prime culture for growth of sin is in the darkness. To combat the infiltration of such a powerful force, many close-knit fellowships purposefully employ a "family meeting" time to give occasion for individuals to express concerns, air grievances, and work out differences. There are no fail-safe formulas for dealing with criticism within the church or fellowship, but on the matters of criticism and secret criticism, we must seek the Lord for guidance.

WE'RE TO BUILD UP, NOT TEAR DOWN

Some Christians mistakenly assume their ability to tear apart a person, suggestion, program, or idea is discernment. But contrary to popular assumption, criticism is not one of the nine gifts of the Holy Spirit. Critical people are prone to complaining, but that is not the purpose of discernment. The Lord gives us discernment to pray. Paul tells us, "Pray in the Spirit at all times and on every occasion. Stay alert and be persistent in your prayers for all believers everywhere" (Eph. 6:18, NLT). Prayer is the most powerful force in the universe to bring about God's purposes. Prayer, not criticism, accomplishes the purposes of heaven here on earth.

Furthermore, the critic who thinks he can discern fault in everything and anything does not benefit the Christian fellowship. People have no need for the critic who negatively judges every plan, action, activity, or person. The critic and faultfinder see the need in a person's life and draws attention to that need or lack. He lives in the negative, putting his finger on everything wrong in the other person but never encouraging that brother or sister toward who God intends that person to be.

Some years ago I terminated a Christian employee over a series of negative incidents after repeatedly correcting him had proved futile. In my exit interview I used the occasion to focus not on his transgressions but on who Christ was calling him to be: a new creation, leaving behind the old man. We discussed his future, his plans, his family, and his relationship with the Lord. He was authentically repentant for his many failures. With his outstanding skills, my support and recommendation, and the grace of God, he called me weeks later to let me know he had landed his dream job. Years later he still holds that position. Today he is a leader in his field and respected by peers. As Christ followers we need to learn to not focus on the failures of others, but rather to call them up higher into His purposes for their life.

If we speak personal words of concern to another brother or sister about them, it is important those words exhort them. The word used in the New Testament for *exhortation* is *paraklēsis*, and it means to entreat or encourage.[3] An exhortation is meant to be an intimate call that comes to encourage, inspire, and motivate the other person in their pursuit of God. If we can't encourage another believer in this manner, then perhaps what we really need to do is simply be silent and repent.

And along those lines, it should be said that just because we think something doesn't mean we should speak it. Fasting words has taught me that the most effective way to deal with my thoughts of criticism is to be silent. Before we ever blurt out a single word of judgment or criticism about a brother or sister, we should take those words to the feet of the cross and allow Jesus to shoulder our sin. He is able. We must repeatedly ask ourselves, "Are these words really beneficial? Will they edify?"

One of the supreme gifts we can give others in the Christian fellowship is the gift of silence. If we practice holding our critical words toward other Christians, we will come into great freedom—a freedom from criticizing and judging—and instead we will have spiritual eyes to see the other person as a unique creation made in our Lord's image.

What would Christ have us do instead of criticize? Love.

THE AUTHORITY TARGET

Unfortunately we make authority figures the target of our worst criticism—and can demonstrate a severe lack of prudence and propriety in this area. While I was sitting in a coffee shop one day, two men walked in talking very loudly, berating their pastor for a dull sermon on Sunday (their evaluation). Their crude, critical comments turned so sour I noticed people in line next to them making faces and turning their backs. The two joked and made critical, sarcastic comments to the point that it was obvious bystanders were cringing with embarrassment. The particular venue where the incident took place wasn't too far from the church where the pastor ministered; it was probable many of those in line knew the pastor or who he was.

What an incredible lack of sensitivity, respect, and civility on the part of these two. They had the role down pat. They were critics to the core. To compound the negative impact of these critics' lack of tact and propriety, it is likely some of those people were cringing not from embarrassment but in criticism of these "followers" of Christ. It is this kind of witness that turns people off to the church and thwarts the work of the Holy Spirit in people's lives.

The level of criticism levied at figures of authority is disgraceful, and Christians seem not to comprehend the damage done when they act like the world with judgments and negative comments about our leaders. When I started the forty-day fast of words, I noticed how quickly I became sensitized to criticism and sarcasm and, in particular, my own criticism and sarcasm. I had to turn off the radio talk shows because they were so critical of our leadership in the country. They are merciless! But it cuts much deeper. I saw how far

I was missing the target in my own attitude toward those in authority. It just seemed the natural thing to do when around others who were making jokes, being sarcastic and critical, to just pile on, chime in with judgments as others lambasted our leaders from the local government to the president. No one was immune. I was numbered among the critics.

What you are going to read right now concerning how Christians are to respond to authority is so important, I pray you slow down and let it descend deep into your soul. We are to pray for those in authority, not criticize and berate them. The future of our nation, our Christian community, and our churches hinges on our prayers as Christians. When we criticize and employ sarcasm instead of prayers and support, we damage the very entities we cherish and want to advance. The familiar passage in 2 Chronicles 7:14 promises us, "If My people, who are called by My name, will humble themselves and pray, and seek My face and turn from their wicked ways, then I will hear from heaven, and will forgive their sin and will heal their land." With so much hanging in the balance, it is time for us to submit to the Lord the words of criticism levied at our leaders, starting now during this forty-day fast of words.

WHAT TO DO WHEN YOU'RE THE TARGET

- Be humble and look for any truth you may need to see in their words.
- Don't try to defend yourself.

- Don't take it personally. A sarcastic and critical person attacks almost everyone; if it wasn't you, it would be someone else.

HOW TO RESPOND

What to do with the critic? We pray for the critic as we pray for ourselves. Most critics have a degree of discernment working in their lives but are in need of personal healing and encouragement. Encourage and participate with the critic in prayer for those individuals or situations they're critical about. It is difficult to criticize and judge those you are praying for. Challenge the critic to use his discernment for prayer and intercession instead. (And if we're the critic, we ought to apply this approach to ourselves!)

How should we respond to sarcasm and criticism? Humility always wins the day. In humility we look for any truth in the words of our critic. We implore the Lord to give us ears to hear, whether it be a slight whisper of truth or a blast of undeniable reality. We must be quick to forgive those who judge and criticize us. As we bring our own critical words to the cross, we must also bring the words of others to the feet of Jesus. We trust that the Lord will use all things for His purposes in our lives—yes, even in the extremes: "The LORD works out everything to its proper end—even the wicked for a day of disaster" (Prov. 16:4, NIV). My experience is that those who have set themselves up as my critic usually have a grain of truth in their criticism that I desperately need to embrace.

Lastly, remember the heart is deceitful. When we speak to another brother about someone else, we are treading on perilous ground. Because our hearts are so deceitful, we don't always know our own intentions and motives. We may think we're seeking another person's help, prayer, or understanding when sharing our concerns about a brother or sister; however, we may actually be walking in deception. Anytime we find ourselves in this kind of covert interaction, we should stop immediately and ask the Lord this question: What would You show me about myself through this?

Chapter 4

LEAVE BEHIND THE PAST—
AND NEGATIVE WORDS

*Negative: thinking about the bad qualities of
someone or something; thinking that a bad result
will happen; not hopeful or optimistic.*[1]

MOST OF US have the propensity to be negative
now and then. However, there are people who are
chronically negative. Negative words that come out of
a believer's mouth are remnants of the life they knew
before coming to know Christ as Savior. They are
the language of the world. But Ephesians 2:19 tells us,
"Now, therefore, you are no longer strangers and for-
eigners, but are fellow citizens with the saints and members of the household of God." As citizens of heaven we
must learn to speak the language of heaven.

Let me remind that you know a person's country
of origin by the language they speak. We have been
raised up with Christ and belong to His kingdom now.
What are the words of His language? Compassionate
words, kind words, encouraging words, and words of
praise and worship—this is the vocabulary of heaven.

In the kingdom of heaven there will be no negative words, no critical or hurtful words. Our Lord
has come to give us freedom from the negative words
that tie us to the past and this world. If we are going
to experience His kingdom on earth, then we must

be free from judging, criticizing, sarcasm, negativity, complaining, and gossip. We need a revelation, a deeper understanding of this issue of negativism and the negative words that cross our lips.

WHAT MAKES US NEGATIVE?

At the time they come to Christ, most people are struggling with a negative self-concept or view of life. Accepting Christ in our hearts makes us a new creation (2 Cor. 5:17). However, we still struggle with our negative behavior and attitudes from the past that linger and prohibit us from seeing ourselves as Christ sees us, as new creations with the old sin and negative bondages gone. For many of us there exists a constant tension of doing what we know we shouldn't do and not doing what we know we should do, of saying what we know we shouldn't say and not saying what we know we should say. It is the struggle that Paul faced and speaks pointedly about in Romans 7:15–20.

I don't believe a Christian can speak the words they should speak until they stop speaking the words they shouldn't speak. This is the reason for the fast. The negative words we say carry so much more weight than the positive words we speak, and they are so damaging.

The truth is, each one of us has a history of negative experiences, and that history is full of negative input from parents, siblings, relationships, friends, acquaintances, schooling, church, work, and other activities. Let's look at the impact a few of these can have on us.

Parents

You may have had parents who made huge mistakes in your upbringing. The truth is, there are no perfect parents, and no matter how much they love their child, parents make mistakes. Young children are tender and vulnerable, and they can be deeply wounded by the negative words spoken by the most significant people in their life: parents. There are very few of us who have not carried around a wound in our hearts from our parents' words, a wound that colors our relationships, particularly our relationships with the opposite sex.

My story is that my father was a World War II veteran and a wonderful, devoted family man. He was a tireless worker and provided for our family. But my dad didn't know how to communicate on an emotional level and rarely issued the words I needed and longed to hear: "I love you. I'm proud of you." Because my dad and I didn't develop an emotional connection, I turned to friends to meet my need for words of affirmation, acceptance, and counsel—and we all know young friends are not usually the best source for wise words of counsel.

Another by-product of my lack of intimacy with my dad was that I didn't have a man to help me with the struggles all young boys go through, and I was vulnerable to negative words and influences. What my dad *did* provide in communication was negative criticism, and he supplied a lot of it. He simply didn't understand the power of negative words—the power of these kinds of phrases:

- "What were you thinking?"
- "If I want something done right, I guess I'll have to do it myself."

Because of my childhood experiences, I judged my father. In judging my father, I set in motion a negative chain of events that caused me to re-create many of my dad's failures and more in my relationship with my sons. It is an all-too-familiar scenario repeated by many of us.

It wasn't until I began the forty-day word fast that I fully understood the power of the negative words and judgments that I had toward my dad. The only response I could give to this revelation was to be broken and repentant before the Lord. When we repent of the judgments and negative words or thoughts we hold against our parents, there comes a new freedom to cut the chains of the past and move into the full identity of who we are in Christ—new creations. We no longer stay prisoners of the past. The negative is gone.

Siblings

Then there's the influence our siblings may have had on us. They may have been overbearing, tormenting, and hurtful in their words and actions. Some social psychologists argue that the most hurtful relationships we can have may be with our siblings, those such as the abusive big brother, the too-perfect sister, or the hypercompetitive sibling of the same sex.[2] As children we speak words that are destructive. We assault one another with demeaning names and vicious verbal attacks. The result of these damaging sibling relationships is a pattern of negative thinking that lapses over into most of our relationships as we grow up. Because of the trauma caused by these siblings' verbal attacks and actions, we judge them and set in motion the negative repercussions judgment always brings.

Bullies

In our culture today young people spend so much time in and out of school with friends and acquaintances that the words spoken in these interactions go far in developing their self-image too. The disparaging names and nicknames used among youth draw them out of childlike attitudes like a magnet and into the land of negativity, where many continue to reside long after a salvation experience. The negative words go deep into the psyche, take root, grow, and give off the fruit of more negative words and negative lifestyles.

Many young people and even adults hear some of the most dreaded words from the mouth of a bully. If you have ever witnessed a bully slap a little boy in the face in front of his friends and then say to the boy, "You measly wimp," then you can understand the brutal humiliation that can come to a person's self-image through a bully. During more than thirty-five years of working with youth and adults in school settings, I have seen few words more damaging to the self-image than those spoken by a bully. Depending on what research you quote, anywhere from 30 percent to 75 percent of all middle and high school kids report being bullied at school or online, and we know young people do not report the majority of bullying experiences.[3] Then there is the cyberbullying and workplace bullying that many adults experience. Oh, the destructive power of the bully's words! I have dealt with the aftermath of the bully's words on more than one occasion, and I've seen that such words can drive a young person to suicide.

I'll share with you an example that went on for weeks. One of our most popular senior girls was spiraling downward in her grades and life. Something was going on, but our administrators and counselors couldn't figure it out. Then, some weeks later, we had an all-school assembly where the girl was on stage and a group of boys started taunting her with a nickname. I called in one of our most outstanding senior boys who had participated in the taunting. It ended up that the young lady had too much to drink at a party and a group of boys took advantage of her. The whole situation was so devastating for all the students involved. The girl ended up having a very serious suicide attempt that took her years to recover from, and the young men's lives were dramatically impacted in many ways. All the parents involved were humiliated and broken. The whole event was heartbreaking.

HOW TO LOVE THE NEGATIVE PERSON IN YOUR LIFE

We do everything we can to avoid negative people. They are simply hard to deal with and impact our state of mind and mood. But sometimes they are our relatives, close friends, church members, or coworkers, and we can't avoid them. Their constant diatribe of pessimism wears us down. They cast a shadow of gloom over even the most positive people and situations. If you try to move forward with some type of positive move in your life, they will tell you why it is going to fail. If you are teaching your daughter to drive, the negative person quips, "You know, thirty-five percent of girls have a serious wreck in their first six months of driving." If you are learning to ski, they respond, "One of my best friends broke his arm and leg the first time he tried to ski." Fulfilling their role of being negative feeds something inside them, and they seem to have a bottomless pit of negative comments.

An additional challenge in relating to negative Christians is that they are often religious. They know all the right words, quote Scripture, and attend church, where they hide in religious functions looking for normalcy and acceptance.

One of the most difficult challenges about being around a chronically negative person is to stand your ground and refuse to allow him or her to affect you personally or cause you to respond negatively. If you are not careful, it is easy to become indifferent to a negative person. Indifference becomes almost like a safety valve in our relationship with the negative person to keep him or her from affecting us. We just dismiss a negative person as having no worth. We make calculated decisions to not share any personal or family challenges we are going through with that negative person, as we know their negative response would be predictable and hurtful.

But the Lord doesn't want us to dismiss a negative person out of hand, though we must use wisdom in what we share with them. They are every bit as much a child of God as we are. We must love, accept, and pray for them. Our challenge with the chronically negative person is to not look at the person's behavior but at what God is calling them to be. They are His children, and He wants them to be free and complete in Him—just as He wants that for us. When we encourage the negative person, then, we don't speak to his or her behavior. We call them up to be the new creations in Christ they are, all things becoming new.

HOW TO RECOGNIZE
NEGATIVITY IN YOURSELF

So, we are often the recipients of negative words from our family, friends, acquaintances, or those we work and fellowship with. Their negative words reinforce our negative self-image. As these negative words pile up on us, we adopt a negative view of life. It becomes our self-talk. You know what I mean. It is all those negative pet names we call ourselves when no one is listening. It is the cursing at yourself when no one is around.

Do you see yourself as a negative person? Do you speak negative words to others? I firmly believe the Lord wants to root out every single negative word from our mouth. He wants joy, rejoicing, and words of life to be coming from our lips, not words of judgment, criticism, sarcasm, complaining, or gossip. Do any of these words sound familiar?

- "You'll never amount to anything."
- "When was the last time you looked in the mirror?"
- "Can you even count to ten?"
- "You look fat in those pants."
- "Can't you do anything right?"

Let's take a look at some questions and thoughts that can help you identify any negativity residing in your life.

Are you quick to say no?

Are you one of those persons who are initially and repeatedly in opposition of just about anything that comes up? When someone brings something new to you, is your first thought to speak words about what can go wrong instead of what can go right? If so, then you may have tendency to be negative. Christ wants us to be so confident in our relationship with Him that others can approach us with new ideas. A negative person is narrow-minded. They do things a particular way because that is the way it has always been done.

Are you unteachable?

Do you see yourself butting up against the same issues in your relationships and life time and time again? Being unteachable is a negative trait that significantly limits your ability to take on more responsibility at work or in other settings. It causes a person to become stagnant and stuck in their spiritual growth and never overcome the same issues of sin they face again and again. Are there multiple people in your life pointing out to you the same issue over and over about yourself that needs to change? Maybe you even call yourself hardheaded. I know so many people who are teachable. They are a joy to approach with a new idea or advice. They are what I call "good receivers"; when the Lord is doing something new, they are first to embrace it. If they need a correction or adjustment in their life, they can hear words of correction and respond positively.

Do you ask forgiveness quickly when you say something hurtful?

Negative people rarely ask forgiveness when they do something wrong. Negative people create tremendous collateral damage around them with their words. They are unable to consider seeking forgiveness from others; it would be overwhelming. To ask forgiveness from others, they would have to assume responsibility for their words and actions. They keep other people in the crosshairs of their negative words so they always have someone to blame. After all, if they can't blame you, then who are they supposed to blame?

Do you find yourself thinking and saying negative thoughts daily?

It could be anything—the weather, the pastor, the church's budget, the color of the carpet at church, or the driver in front of you. Most damaging of all is the way negative people see relationships in a negative light. The telling sign of a negative person is the state of their relationships. They are negative about the world in which they live. They are negative about the church. They reside in the shadow land of eternal pessimism.

Negative people may be timid or aggressive, but they are full of anxiety and worry a lot. They have issues trusting other people. They're fearful. Fearful words are the enemy's favorite words. Satan delights in Christians operating out of fear and speaking words of fear. When we live and speak in fear, the enemy is in his glory. He can communicate with us when we're in that state. He can influence our words, our decisions, and our lives.

Do you act out the drama triangle?

A negative person perpetually lives in the drama triangle and vacillates between all its roles. As *perpetrator* the negative person gets a feeling of safety by speaking words that hurt others and speaking put-downs. The negative person swells with feelings of superiority as he or she lords it over others with negative comments. Negative people are a master at issuing words to blame and attack others. As *victim* the negative person finds safety in being submissive. As the victim he or she wallows in self-pity and exhibits passive aggressive behavior. The victim is a master of manipulation. As *rescuer* the negative person feels superior to others because he or she sacrifices more and is highly judgmental of others. The negative person acting out the role of rescuer has anger issues and feels a strong sense of entitlement. They strike back at authority when they don't get what they think is deserved.

Do you have a disapproving air about you?

Of the many negative words, actions, and non-verbal communications the negative person emits, disapproval bears special attention. A negative person has a certain mastery of that infamous look of disapproval. We all have felt its sting at one time or another. Most of us have heard those words of disapproval: "What were you thinking?" That's another way of saying, "Are you stupid?"

If you grow up under a cloud of disapproving words and looks from a parent, you will probably rain on the parade of others for many years. Disapproval from parents, friends, and significant others robs a person of self-confidence. It creates a skewed perception of God. Those who live under the cloud of disapproval see God through a negative paradigm that says, "You deserved that beating you got. You asked for it when you dressed that way."

WHAT TO DO ABOUT BEING NEGATIVE

The Lord has another way for us. Through Him we can conquer all things. He wants to bring us freedom from negative words and launch us into His purposes. This launching becomes difficult when we hold on to negative traits and words in our life from the past. Our Lord wants to bring His kingdom into our midst, His kingdom that is full of thanksgiving and joy.

So, what are we to do about this negative part of our lives? How do we respond to it and overcome it?

It's challenging to rid our lives of the negative residue that resides in us. The negative part of you will always come back, saying, "This is too difficult; no one can do this," or, "You can't escape that trap you're in." This powerful negativity will always exert itself when God begins to call us up to a higher place in Him, and He is always calling us up higher (2 Cor. 3:18).

Conquering the negative patterns in our lives requires a reversal in our interpretation of life and how we see life. It requires a new paradigm. We have to stop seeing life through negative glasses and begin to see it through spiritual eyes that are positive, hopeful, and looking to the potential for growth in Christ in all things. It is not just the huge life-changing events that we need to see and hear differently. It is the everyday negative experiences that we encounter that the Lord wants to use to change us.

Here's an example. I had just finished lunch with a mentor and was sharing what the Lord was showing me about how He uses all of the events in our life for His purposes. My friend suggested we go back to his place to visit. He led the way to his new home and I followed. When we arrived, he confessed to me how frustrated he became with the car in front of him that was driving so slow. He was starting to boil over, wondering what was going on with this person. Then he felt a tug on his heart and knew the Lord wanted him to have more patience. He told me he repented right then and asked the Lord to forgive him. I said to my friend that one of the great tests of life is patience; it is about trusting the Lord with His timing. The Lord has no conception of time. He has all the time in the world. He wants us to trust Him; that is what patience is about. And I told my mentor, "Congratulations, you passed the test."

We need to put to death the negative spirit within us. We need to stop feeding it. In this endeavor the first task we have to accomplish is to wholly accept that our flesh has nothing to offer in the pursuit of living in the spirit. Our flesh is fed by living in the negative experiences and the words of this world. There really is only one answer to the flesh: it needs to die!

Ridding our lives of negativity is not a self-help program for the flesh. There is nothing worth renewing in our flesh that can make it somehow positive and cause it to yearn after life in the spirit. Our flesh rails against the Spirit-filled life that leaves no room for negativity and its language. Galatians 5:17 says, "For the flesh desires what is contrary to the Spirit, and the Spirit what is contrary to the flesh. They are in conflict with each other, so that you are not to do whatever you want" (NIV). This point is clarified also in John 6:63, where Jesus says, "It is the Spirit who gives life. The flesh profits nothing. The words that I speak to you are spirit and are life."

As we partake of the forty-day word fast, we will rid our lives of these negative words that constrain our spiritual growth, make us prisoners of the past, and damage our relationships. We will begin to see life through the eyes of the Spirit. We will begin to see our experiences from God's perspective. With God all things work together and are good. We are assured of this in 1 Corinthians 12:6: "There are various operations, but it is the same God who operates all of them in all people."

As we look at the entirety of our experiences through the eyes of the Spirit, we realize that He orchestrates the negative events and words in our life and weaves them into His plans. He uses them for good. He brings glory to His name through them. Again this idea is supported in Proverbs: "The LORD has made all things for Himself, yes, even the wicked for the day of evil." (Prov. 16:4). No experience is outside of God's template to beckon us up to greater faith and trust in Him:

- Financial pressures are a call to trust Him for provision and take a step up in faith that He is Jehovah Jireh, our provider: "God shall supply your every need according to His riches in glory by Christ Jesus" (Phil. 4:19).
- Unjust treatment by others becomes one of the greatest opportunities for Christian maturity we can have—the chance to participate in the fellowship of His sufferings: "But rejoice insofar as you share in Christ's sufferings, so that you may rejoice and be glad also in the revelation of His glory" (1 Pet. 4:13).

- If someone steals from us, we have the wonderful opportunity to show him or her the
  love of Jesus: "To him who strikes you on
  the one cheek, offer also the other. And from
  him who takes away your cloak, do not with-
  hold your tunic as well" (Luke 6:29). Also,
  "But love your enemies, and do good, and
  lend, hoping for nothing in return. Then
  your reward will be great, and you will be the
  sons of the Highest. For He is kind to the
  unthankful and the evil" (Luke 6:35).

- Rebellious children are poignant opportunities to see the power of God work on our
  behalf through prayer. They are the living
  experiences for us of His faithfulness: "But
  this is what the LORD says: 'Yes, captives
  will be taken from warriors, and plunder
  retrieved from the fierce; I will contend with
  those who contend with you, and your children I will save'" (Isa. 49:25, NIV).

- Situations that we used to respond to with
  frustration are calls for greater patience in
  the spirit of Paul's words: "Be anxious for
  nothing, but in everything, by prayer and
  supplication with gratitude, make your
  requests known to God. And the peace of
  God, which surpasses all understanding,
  will protect your hearts and minds through
  Christ Jesus" (Phil. 4:6–7).

When the negative words are gone from our life, we are free to stop asking why. *Why* is a question of fear. It is a question in search of blame. It is a question that reveals a lack of trust in our Lord. The Lord wants to know that He can trust us to wait on Him in all experiences. We know longer ask *why*; we ask *what*. If you want to get the right answer, you must ask the right question. You now ask, "What do You want me to learn from this, Lord? What do You want to accomplish in my life? What is my part in this, Lord? What do You want my response to be?"

As we fast for forty days, we will be putting an end to all those negative words that have marred our relationships. We will be putting to death the things of the earthly, worldly nature. Paul describes it this way: of which Paul calls malice, slander, and filthy language, abusive language, and all forms of negative words.

> Therefore put to death the parts of your earthly nature: sexual immorality, uncleanness, inordinate affection, evil desire, and covetousness, which is idolatry.
> —COLOSSIANS 3:5

> But now you also, put them all aside: anger, wrath, malice, slander, and abusive speech from your mouth.
> —COLOSSIANS 3:8, NAS

As we embrace daily the forty-day word fast, we will starve these negative words into oblivion, and there will be no fertile soil in our life for them. We will create a spiritual immune system that is strong and vibrant and that insulates us from the negative words of the world. We will be on guard, always vigilant to hear God's words of instruction and direction about every situation that challenges us to trust Him more. We will come to understand that He is in all things: "For from Him and through Him and to Him are all things. To Him be glory forever! Amen" (Rom. 11:36).

Chapter 5

THE POISON OF COMPLAINT

Complain: to lament; to utter expressions of resentment;
to murmur; to find fault, to utter expressions of pain.

PEOPLE COMPLAIN. PEOPLE complain about almost everything and anything. However, in the act of complaining, we create an atmosphere, an air around us that cannot host the presence of the Lord. Grumbling, murmuring, whining—whatever synonym you want to ascribe to complaining, they all have the same effect. They quench the Spirit of the Lord. Again, the language of heaven is thanksgiving, praise, and gratefulness. Complaining isn't the language the Lord speaks; it's not in His vocabulary.

I believe complaining disconnects our line of communication to the Lord. It's akin to taking a pair of snips and cutting a telephone cable cleanly into two pieces. No signal can transmit to the Lord. He doesn't hear our prayers. Furthermore, that disconnect works in two ways—not only does the Lord not hear our prayers, but also the person who complains can't hear the Lord. When you are living in a complaining attitude, you simply can't hear the Lord.

WHAT'S YOUR POISON?

What is your weapon of choice when it comes to complaining? There are so many variations to choose from. We can:

- Murmur
- Disapprove
- Express dislike
- Whine
- Carp
- Grouse
- Sound off
- Blame
- Pity ourselves
- Grumble
- Make a fuss
- Bleat
- Snivel
- Beef
- Raise a stink
- Fault-find
- Gripe
- Lament
- Depreciate
- Nag
- Wail
- Bellyache
- Fret
- Protest
- Impute

As you can see, the ways to complain are never-ending. It is part of our human condition. However, it affects everyone around us. Complaining is like emotional pollution; it pollutes the air we breathe and the environment around all others. It sends an emotional virus into the air that others breathe and become infected with. It spreads like sneezing into the air and is only limited by how far the words can be heard. If we complain about the president, many people will join in. If we complain about the economy, we will have myriads of takers piling on. If we complain about the past, we will have others commiserate with us in louder complaints. We complain about just anything.

WHAT WE LOVE TO COMPLAIN ABOUT

Let's face it; there's always something we can complain about. And wow, do we love to complain! Here's just a short list of the contenders. We complain about:

- Our jobs
- Our bosses
- The weather
- Mondays
- Getting up in the morning
- People who drive too close
- People who drive too fast
- Customer service
- Slow Internet
- No toilet paper

- Our siblings
- The way people smell
- Toll roads
- Our children
- Our hair
- Our spouses
- Our pastors
- Our worship leaders
- Inconsiderate people
- Waiting in line

COMPLAINING OR CRYING OUT?

No one wants to be known as a whiner. We don't want to come to the Lord with our requests as disgruntled, grumbling, or complaining sons and daughters either. There is a legitimate difference between our lamentations before the Lord born out of sorrow, grief, and need and the self-centered complaints drawn from issues of entitlement and ingratitude. The Lord wants us to come before Him with all of our emotional expressions. When we face repeated difficulties or prayers that are not answered, our Father in heaven expects us to cry out to Him: "In my distress I called on the Lord, and cried for help to my God; He heard my voice from His temple, and my cry for help came before Him to His ears" (Ps. 18:6).

When we cry out to the Lord time and time again, what makes this different than complaining is that we are not just bringing our petitions, hurts, and intercessions for others to Him. We are also saying, "What do You want to teach me?" It's not a question of, "Why is this happening, Lord?" It's more a matter of, "Help me."

THE SILENT COMPLAINT

We know our hearts are deceitful, and because of this deceit we may find ourselves looking for validation in our pain. Even when we think we have our words under control, we may find ourselves wallowing in self-pity and complaining through nonverbal actions and sounds.

I'm intimately acquainted with this. After suffering in very serious pain for five years, I began to take a turn for the better through some unusual and surprising treatment. It was challenging for me to let go of many of the habitual patterns of behavior I had incorporated into my life to cope with my pain. I noticed one particular action was hard to let go of: groaning. I still had pain, and I still groaned in pain.

What's wrong with groaning? After all, you groan when you're in pain. Right? Well, I began to notice I *didn't* groan in pain when I was alone. You see, when we suffer with just about anything, the people close to us suffer also. And we control how much those people suffer. Whether it's losing a job or a traumatic illness, we control how much those around us suffer with us. When we are in self-pity or feeling sorry for ourselves, we feel validated or somehow better about our situation if we know others understand just how bad we really have it, how unjustly we were treated, how unappreciated we are, how much pain we are in, and on and on.

When I began to let go of the groaning and other nonverbal actions I used to seek validation through my pain, I began to release my wife from suffering with me.

Someone coined the phrase *injustice collectors* to describe people who live in self-pity. These people number and catalog every injustice done to them and then search until they can find someone to sympathize with them. People wallow in self-pity because they have a low self-esteem, and they are searching for validation from others. They seek validation through negative words and behavior. In essence, they are on the search to find someone who will feel sorry for them. This validates their victim mentality that continually allows them to escape taking responsibility for their life.

Self-pity is a way of complaining that paralyzes any person who employs its use. When you find yourself moving toward self-pity in difficult circumstances, do what is the only proper response: stomp on its head!

The truth is we are all challenged to our core at one time or another with painful experiences. We can complain and make others suffer with us in a myriad of ways. Or we can quietly, with faith, trust our Lord. Can we be patient and trust the Lord? Can we trust Him for provision? Can we trust Him for a spouse? Can we trust Him with our children?

Conversely I believe the Lord wants to be able to trust us. So, what does He do? He tests us. He tests us ever so thoroughly. Just as He tested the Israelites, He tests us. Moses said to the people, "Do not fear, for God has come to test you, so that the fear of Him may be before you so that you do not sin" (Exod. 20:20).

When difficult circumstances come our way, we can complain in numerous ways to an untold number of people. We can get others to feel sorry for us. We can collect a contingency of backers who will support us, or we can choose to trust our Lord who is good. He takes anything that others meant for evil in our lives and uses it for His purposes.

THE POWER OF GROUP GRUMBLING

If you haven't had the experience of working in a place of business like an office, school, or organization where there were a lot of grumblers, then you should thank the Lord. It can be quite the challenging experience. A group of grumblers can drown out even the most positive people.

Here is an experience I had with it. At one occasion in my career I took over the leadership of an inner city high school that was left in disarray by a combination of failed leadership, a student body wrecked by gangs and fighting, and a teaching staff that was on its own. The staff felt unsupported and unappreciated. The football team had a twenty-plus-game losing streak, going zero wins and ten losses two years in a row. Things really couldn't get a lot worse, I thought. Enter the new principal fresh to the high school scene. Within the first year we had a shooting where five girls were shot at lunchtime, one of them five times (thankfully no one died), ending up with an environment fertile for grumbling.

The school had teacher representative grumblers, department chair grumblers, tenured teacher grumblers, class officer grumblers, PTA grumblers, student body officer grumblers, and even administrative grumblers. There were some outstanding faculty members and students, but they were dwarfed by the grumbling masses. That's the way grumbling works; the loudest grumblers drown out the most positive of people.

I'm going to tell you how this story ends. In fact, God used it to teach me the antidote to a grumbling and complaining spirit. But before I do, let's turn to some of the most skilled complainers we have record of—the children of Israel—and see what they teach us about complaining.

ISRAEL'S BITTER ROOTS

If there's any group that can model for us the negative power of complaint, it's Israel. At one point in their history, we read, "The whole congregation of the children of Israel murmured against Moses and Aaron in the wilderness" (Exod. 16:2). Wait a minute, the whole community? The whole community numbered approximately two million people, counting women and children! (See Numbers 1:45–46.) That's quite a troupe of grumblers.

And, oh, what a history with grumbling they had. First the Israelites grumbled as Pharaoh pursued them to the edge of the sea. They said to Moses, "Is it because there were no graves in Egypt that you have taken us away to die in the wilderness? Why have you dealt with us in this way, bringing us out of Egypt?" (Exod. 14:11). Then the whole community grumbled about the report of the spies concerning the Promised Land (Num. 14:36). They grumbled too about the bitter water (Exod. 15:23–24).

It finally came to a head in Exodus 16:2, where the whole group of two million people were grumbling against Moses. Never mind that they had seen God open up the Red Sea and rescue them the first time they grumbled or that they had just seen the bitter waters at Marah instantly made sweet at their continued grumbling. Now the whole community was grumbling for no other reason than that their supplies were getting low and they didn't like the desert.

What follows in Exodus 16:2–34 is a centerpiece of understanding that will help us comprehend why we complain and what these complaining words mean to God. Please take the time to read this entire section in Exodus.

WHY DO WE COMPLAIN?

Despite the incredible blessings and interventions of God that they had just seen, the children of Israel had forgotten where they were headed. They lost their way. The truth is, they could not be satisfied with just each day's provision.

When we complain, we blind ourselves to all the good things the Lord has accomplished in us and for us. By complaining, we disavow all of God's past provision and His hopes and promises for the future. We doubt the very faithfulness of God. In short, complaining is doubting God is who He says He is. We doubt He is good. It measures all of God's promises to us and finds them wanting because of one immediate situation of need we have. Complaining is an action that says to God, "I don't have faith in You. I don't trust You. I don't really believe You are good."

Complaining sends all the wrong messages to God, and that is exactly what Israel did in the desert. After the whole community grumbled about their month's provision of food running low, God decided to feed them with quail in the evening and manna in the morning. He gave them explicit instructions about gathering the food from heaven, and He even made provision for gathering on the day before the Sabbath by supplying enough for two days so they could have a Sabbath rest. Yet in spite of all His faithfulness, forgiveness, and blessing, the Israelites could not trust Him and be obedient. They kept leftovers for the next morning, not trusting the manna would fall again. They came out on the Sabbath looking for more food.

We see in this example of the children of Israel the two foundational reasons we speak complaining words as Christians:

1. Entitlement. We're ungrateful for what we have and think we deserve more.

2. Ingratitude. We don't trust in God's goodness.

THE WILDFIRE SPREAD OF INGRATITUDE

I wonder if our ingratitude catches the Lord's attention as it does ours as parents. There are few things that rankle an adult like an ungrateful child. It stings so intensely because it is often aimed toward one who has made so much sacrifice for us. Probably every one of us has felt that pain of our generous gift, gesture, or work going unappreciated.

It is critically important for us to recognize that complaining and grumbling have their roots and beginning in ingratitude. Ingratitude is not just some passing attitude, something that is trivial. Rather, it is a serious heart issue that has major consequences in our lives.

The ingratitude of the children of Israel was a sin embedded deep within their hearts, and it came flooding out in complaints and grumbling. Ingratitude and our tongue have a common denominator: they both produce results that are dramatically greater than we could ever conceive. The words of complaint that crossed the tongues of the children of Israel kept them out of the Promised Land. For us, the tongue can burn up everything around us: "The tongue is a fire, a world of evil. The tongue is among the parts of the body, defiling the whole body, and setting the course of nature on fire, and it is set on fire by hell" (James 3:6).

It may seem hard to get your theology around this concept, but ingratitude can lead to a paradigm of thought that is so perverse the Lord eventually gives the person over to it and pursues him no more. Romans 1 teaches, "Yes, they knew God, but they wouldn't worship him as God or even give him thanks. And they began to think up foolish ideas what God was like. As a result, their minds became dark and confused.... That is why God abandoned them to their shameful desires" (Rom. 1:21, 26, NLT).

IS GOD REALLY GOOD?

The words that we speak answer this question: Is God really good? The Israelites' words showed they repeatedly questioned the goodness of God. No matter how He saved them or what He provided, they always assumed their next experience would be negative. Their words gave themselves away; they did not expect God to be good to them.

Why is questioning God's goodness such a huge sin? To deny God's goodness is to recant the very nature and glory of God. When Moses found favor with God and asked to see His glory, this is how the Lord responded: "Then He said, 'I will make all My goodness pass before you, and I will proclaim the name of the LORD before you. I will be gracious to whom I will be gracious and will show mercy on whom I will show mercy'" (Exod. 33:19). In denying God's goodness, we are denying His very existence as one who is merciful and compassionate.

How to Overcome Complaining

Back to that high school. There was so much complaining going on at the high school, you would have thought it was the wilderness experience of the Israelites. I began to see that we really had some fine young people and faculty. Our band was one of the best marching bands in the city. And our girls' fast-pitch softball team won the state championship to start the year.

Two small things turned the tide around in just a matter of months. First, we started a brag sheet and drew attention to every good thing that was going on at the school. Second, we let parents know about it. We stopped letting the negative words and complaining at the school drown out all the positives that were also going on. I passed down an edict: every Friday teachers had to hand in with their lesson plans at least one positive handwritten note about a student, and we mailed those notes home every week. The reaction from parents and the community was wild. Many of the parents said it was the first positive interaction they had ever had with the school. An encouraging, positive, handwritten note from one of their children's teachers stunned them. And you know where most of those notes went? Right up on the refrigerator for everyone to see who came into the house. In a few short months parent attitudes began to change about the school. We were on a roll. Why?

Because the antithesis of complaining is gratefulness. It is finding something to be thankful about. Yes, I had some hard-core complaining teachers who said they couldn't find one thing positive about any of their 140 students. They came around slowly.

Gratefulness, thanksgiving, praise to God for who He is and what He has done for us—all of these expressions send a message to God that resonates with His Spirit. How do you overcome evil? With good. There is always good somewhere, and no matter how dark the day seems, God is able to show His love, compassion, and care for us in many ways. We simply have to be on the lookout for it.

So, how do you overcome complaining? Focus on the many good things our Lord has provided for you. Our message is to be that of the psalmist: "I will bless the Lord at all times; His praise will continually be in my mouth" (Ps. 34:1). Instead of grumbling and complaining, we are to praise God for His goodness to us. Praise to God—acclamation, appreciation, adoration, and applause—should be the very words continually on our lips.

Chapter 6

THE MOST WICKED OF ALL WORDS

Gossip: sharing information with someone about a problem or another person when that person we are sharing it with is not part of the problem or part of the solution to the problem.

THERE ARE FEW words in our English language that arouse the spectrum of emotions as the word *gossip*. Just hearing it can provoke anger, fear, rage, embarrassment, and pity, to name just some of the obvious—anger when we see the impact of it, fear that it could happen to us, rage when it does happen to us, embarrassment when we hear it used to broadcast a friend's failure to others, and pity when we see the damage it does to an innocent person.

Gossip is a natural part of the world in which we live. Turn on the news any day, and you will hear salacious words about politicians, movie stars, even the pope. No one is immune from gossip.

However, gossip is not limited to figures of notoriety. We hear words of gossip about our children's teachers at school, our friends, members of our church, and even our pastors. Gossip is deeply embedded in the language of this world. To exacerbate the craziness and damage of gossip, there are whole industries built around it. The paparazzi industry has become a major force in the entertainment industry and news. With the advent of social media and new technologies for intruding on people's privacy, juicy gossip is readily available, 24/7. Just choose your source—gossip websites, gossip magazines, gossip blogs. One source even brags, "Gossip updated every 10 minutes 24/7."[1]

The words of a gossip are the most wicked of all words. Why? Gossiping carries great negative, destructive power. It does more damage that lasts longer and spreads further than other negative words. Gossip creates its own life, gaining momentum, expanding in influence as it broadcasts among people, with each person adding their negative spin upon it. One act of gossip can tarnish or ruin a person's lifelong, hard-earned, good reputation. A gossipy remark can decimate someone's self-image and self-confidence. Gossip can lead to alienation, depression, and the loss of lifelong friends. It can lead to divorce or suicidal thoughts. It can destroy a pastor, his ministry, and his church.

I believe we can only comprehend the depth and scope of gossip through spiritual understanding. How important is it for us to understand gossip, not participate in it, and guard ourselves against it? Proverbs 6:16–19 is specific about that:

> These six things the LORD hates, yes, seven are
> an abomination to him: a proud look, a lying
> tongue, and hands that shed innocent blood,
> a heart that devises wicked imaginations, feet
> that are swift in running to mischief, a false
> witness who speaks lies, and he who sows dis-
> cord among brethren.

Pay very close attention to the seventh item that God despises—the spreading of deception among brothers. Why is that particular sin so grievous? Because unity in the Christian community is what Christ sought for all believers. Unity was His repeated prayer to the Father in John 17:22–23, otherwise known as the High Priestly Prayer. He prayed to the Father, "I have given them the glory that you gave me, that they may be one as we are one—I in them and you in me—so that they may be brought to complete unity. Then the world will know that you sent me and have loved them even as you have loved me" (NIV). Unity among believers is what Christ believed would draw people to Him.

WHAT TYPE OF GOSSIP ARE YOU?

While we would all agree that gossip is strongly spoken against in the Scriptures, most of us still find it challenging to not listen to, spread, or sometimes even start the gossip train. But listening to gossip and participating in it reveals our sinful heart. Taking part in it exposes our poverty of spiritual wisdom and understanding and our lack of love for other believers.

Gossip is subtle, enticing, and addictive, and it can easily snare a person. We can be caught participating in it—from spreading simple rumors to entering the dark depths of slander. How are you a member of the gossip train?

The rumormonger

You hear something negative about a person and know that it might not be true, so you casually mention it to someone else, hoping to clarify what you heard and get more information. There it goes—the rumor mill has begun, and you turned the crank a little more. For you, God's word is, "Do not spread false reports. Do not help a guilty person by being a malicious witness" (Exod. 23:1, NIV).

The busybody

When a person has too much free time, in their idleness and boredom they can find excitement by keeping tabs on everybody else. They keep their well filled by listening hard in small prayer groups. They surf websites about the failures of Christian ministers, looking for more gossip they can learn about others. This passage is meant for them: "We hear that some among you are idle and disruptive. They are not busy; they are busybodies" (2 Thess. 3:11, NIV).

The grumbler

Grumblers are the ones who wait until a person leaves the room and then criticizes him or her. They covertly complain and spread strife. They undermine and attack authority with their grumbling words, all in the guise of just sharing their opinion. They love to say, "Excuse me, I just need to vent." Maybe this describes you. If so, heed these words: "A perverse person stirs up conflict, and a gossip separates close friends" (Prov. 16:28, NIV).

The slanderer

Call it slander, libel, or backstabbing, it all has one goal: to destroy others. Slander is malicious and deliberately false information. God speaks through His Word a very stern warning against such behavior: "Whoever secretly slanders his neighbor, him I will destroy; no one who has a haughty look and an arrogant heart will I endure" (Ps. 101:5, NAS).

WHY DO PEOPLE GOSSIP?

> The words of a gossip are like choice morsels;
> they go down to the inmost parts.
> —PROVERBS 26:22, NIV

Gossip is sin, and our hearts can be wicked and put forth wicked words when we are not following Christ. It is easier for us to recognize gossip when it is horribly slanderous about a person's sex life, or just not believable in its sensational exaggeration about a person's past. We can recognize and distance ourselves from these words quite fast. But what about that little guilty pleasure of the supermarket tabloid headline or the eavesdropping we might do on other people's conversations or the latest news we might seek out about our neighbors? We are enticed and carried away by our flesh into sin. There is something about gossip that is unsavory yet appealing to our flesh. That is why we gossip—it appeals to our flesh.

I have always believed when you are in authentic fellowship with other Christians, there are distinct, telltale signs. Confidentiality is practiced. Matthew 18 is followed in dealing with conflict. And then this most interesting interaction takes place: people become excited when others become successful.

When my daughter and son-in-law were in their third year of medical residency, my daughter had a chief resident who was quite the wise person. Residency is one of the most difficult experiences any person can endure, filled with eighty-hour workweeks and low pay. Many residents feel like they are being used for slave labor. All the ingredients are there for a very negative environment where people might complain, gossip, and grumble. But the chief resident pulled all the residents together and said, "We are going to practice positive gossip. Any time you hear something positive said about another person, gossip it to everyone; that's the only type of gossip allowed."

When we talk about other people, do we talk about their successes or failures? Answer this question to yourself: What do I find more interesting and what draws my attention more, a person's failures or a person's job promotion? When you are of the world, you speak the world's language and delight more in a person's failures than successes. When you are of the kingdom of our Lord, you delight in other's successes.

ALL KINDS OF GOSSIP

If you could take a snapshot of gossip, you would have to take many different pictures. There's more than one kind of gossip. Let's take a closer look at the different ways this insidious speech permeates conversation.

Slander

> But now you must also rid yourselves of all
> such things as these: anger, rage, malice,
> slander, and filthy language from your lips.
> —Colossians 3:8, niv

> Whoever slanders their neighbor in secret,
>   I will put to silence;
> whoever has haughty eyes and a proud heart,
>   I will not tolerate.
> —Psalm 101:5, niv

As mentioned earlier, slander is spreading information about someone that is not true. From a worldly
standpoint, if you do this in writing, our law calls it
libel. In either case, a person can cause serious damage
to another person's reputation, career, or marriage.

When it comes to slander or libel and the law, ignorance is not an alibi. If you repeat a rumor you heard
or put it in writing and it's not true, you are liable if
it causes damages. But that is the law of the land. We
have a higher standard as Christians, and the Word's
instruction is unquestionable. We are to put it away
from us.

Talebearing

> A talebearer revealeth secrets: but he that is of a
> faithful spirit concealeth the matter.
> —Proverbs 11:13, kjv

One who goes about revealing secrets and repeating matters is a talebearer. In the King's James Version the word *gossip* is not mentioned once, but the word *talebearer* is used numerous times. A talebearer never confronts the person about a rumor he or she has heard. They never go directly to a person if they have offense against the person. A talebearer uncovers others' private issues and does it in secret—a deadly combination.

Whispering

> And even as they did not like to retain God in their knowledge, God gave them over to a reprobate mind, to do those things which are not convenient; being filled with all unrighteousness, fornication, wickedness, covetousness, maliciousness; full of envy, murder, debate, malignity; whisperers.
>
> —ROMANS 1:28–29, KJV

Whispering can include gossip, lies, slander, talebearing, and many other types of defaming words spoken about another person. However, they are conveyed in a particular manner that set it apart as diabolical and evil. It is done with the intent to have the person delivering the evil words not discovered as the messenger. The whisperer does it ever so quietly and in a manner so as not to be identified as the gossiping party. Beware the whisperer.

What to Do When Someone Gossips to You

He who goes about as a slanderer reveals secrets,
Therefore do not associate with a gossip.
—Proverbs 20:19, NAS

Because of the many different levels and types of gossip, it is easy to be deceived into measuring it as being more or less egregious given the nature of the gossip and the situation. We insert in a conversation, for example, the fact that a mutual friend just had their car repossessed. Or we just happen to mention that our friends we fellowship with are contemplating getting separated. We fail to mention that they told us with the intention for us to pray for them, and they said nothing about giving us permission to share it with others. More juicy gossip, such repeating to someone else a friend's sexual failure, is often viewed in the proper light as being off-limits and sinful; however, we repeatedly fail to recognize the subtle nuances of less salacious gossip and its damaging impact and sinful nature.

All of these forms of gossip have become a normal part of our lives for many reasons, primarily because we make mistakes and sin. However, another major reason we experience these negative words in action is because we do not follow the Scriptures in addressing them. How should we approach daily interactions within the Christian community when these negative words are in operation in our midst?

Through the years, time and time again, I've heard

people say, "Just follow Matthew 18. That's all you need to do." But I've found it a challenge to find what that really means. What is the model of Matthew 18, really? I believe if we clearly understand it, it shows us how to deal with gossip, judging, and all other forms of negative words that harm our fellowship.

So, first, confidentiality is the key issue in addressing gossip: "If your brother or sister sins, go and point out their fault, just between the two of you" (Matt. 18:15, NIV). If someone is gossiping to us or we become aware they are spreading words of slander or criticism behind the backs of others, we are not to listen to them and are to confront them in private. Yes, we are to pray for them, but we have the responsibility to confront them in private too.

When we do not practice confidentiality in addressing issues, communicating, resolving complaints or concerns, or sharing information, we separate people and plant seeds of strife. Scripture is clear in this passage. It does not say share your concern with another person initially, get other people's ideas on the matter, or make it a matter of prayer in the prayer group.

Please read these words carefully and with an open heart. One of the more prevalent forms of gossip in the church takes place in prayer groups. Most of us have experienced it at one time or another. Gossip is shared in the name of "getting all the information so we know how to pray right." This is unnecessary because God already knows the need and doesn't require us to remind Him with the minutiae.

Confidentiality is the extreme opposite of gossip. If we establish a community of people who support, reinforce, and teach confidentiality, we will create an atmosphere of trust and confidence. This is the kind of community people will want to be a part of.

Please hear this serious word of caution about listening to gossip. The Scriptures are explicit: do not associate with a gossip. If we do not associate with a gossip, we cannot hear his or her words. So what do we do when someone gossips to us? Leave. Don't associate with him. Yes, again, you can confront the person, but nothing is to be gained by listening to his gossip. However, there a great deal to be lost if you stay.

Gossip influences you even if you are a person who has chosen to not to gossip. It is insidious; its words go deep into a person's spirit.

It's particularly important for pastors and their families and counselors to be especially careful to turn away from gossip. In their position it's not uncommon for people to come to them with complaints and gossip. The truth is when you listen to gossip, it colors your thoughts concerning the person being gossiped about. It influences your perception of them. It is very difficult when you see that person gossiped about to not consider the gossip you have heard.

For example, a close friend once told me about an employee he had to discipline for not doing his job. Wouldn't you know it, years later my wife and I ended up in a home fellowship group with the man and his wife. In the back of my mind I was always thinking he must not be a responsible person. I had listened to gossip, and my thoughts about this man were negative. As we got to know the couple, however, I began to understand the dramatic and tragic life challenges the two of them had faced and overcome; they are amazing people. I discovered they are very hard-working, responsible, and exceptional. Today they are very successful with their own private business.

I thought I could listen to just a little gossip and it wouldn't affect me. I was wrong. No matter how mature a person, you cannot listen to gossip and not be affected. That is the very nature of gossip; it is sin, it affects people deeply.

COVERING OR COVERING UP?

Ultimately one of the most important lessons we can ever learn about relating to our brothers and sisters in Christ is the importance of covering another believer's sin and failures. By doing this, we show the depth and authenticity of our love for one another.

Peter instructs us, "Above all, love each other deeply, because love covers a multitude of sins" (1 Pet. 4:8, NIV). This verse instructs us to recognize that when we reveal another believer's sin or failures, we are uncovering them. Gossiping, then, is in direct opposition to 1 Peter 4:8. If we become aware of another Christian's past failures or negative issues, love demands that we cover and not repeat that information to anyone.

Conversely have you ever been involved in a cover-up? What does it mean to cover up as opposed to covering another's sin? Early in my working career I was put in a situation where the authority over me pressured me to not reveal some practices in the area we worked that were very questionable. In my immaturity and lack of wisdom I rationalized that I was operating in obedience under the authority placed over me. Years later I realized I had been involved in a cover-up. I was covering up someone's sin that was probably illegal and obscuring important information the final authority over the area had a right and need to know.

When we are involved in keeping something from coming to light that is directly against policies, procedures, or the law in a particular area, we are covering up. For example, you are working for a large organization and they have specific policies for travel reimbursement. Supervising this area is one of your areas of responsibility. You become aware of a Christian brother who is padding his travel reimbursements regularly and significantly. What do you do? Do you treat him differently because he is a Christian? Obviously you should pray. Then, based on my experience and Scripture, I would go to him and let him know I was aware of his indiscretions and give him the opportunity to confess his falsehood to the company. If he didn't, then I would need to report him. If you do just about anything else, you are covering up an indiscretion. *Covering up*, then, is when you stand in the way of someone knowing information he has a right and need to know.

We have clearly established in 1 Peter 4:8, on the other hand, that the Lord expects us to cover a brother or sister's sin and not reveal personal information that we know. It is fitting that Peter includes the word *multitude* in this verse. He's saying that this verse has broad application. There are a lot of different ways to sin, and people have repeated failures. We are to cover them all, not picking one sin over another, and *covering them* means not repeating them to anyone.

Gossip can be as simple as sharing negative information with someone about another person when that someone has no need to know it. Therein lies the heart of gossip—involving others where they just don't need to be involved, sharing information with others when they don't need to know the information and wouldn't be part of the solution to the problem anyway.

That means gossip can include something that is true about a person. However, just because something is true doesn't make the information prudent to be shared. Can you feel the sting of gossip in these statements?

- "Did you know he had been married before?"
- "I understand he went bankrupt twice."
- "You know she had a nervous breakdown some years ago."

We're not to be involved with any of this. We are meant to prefer each other and outdo one another in showing each other honor. When it comes to our relationships with other believers, we are admonished to go out of our way to make sure the words that come out of our mouth show honor and respect.

Chapter 7

FIND THE MORE EXCELLENT WAY

Yet I will show you a more excellent way...
—1 CORINTHIANS 12:31

IT IS EASY to get stuck at a particular place in life and for that place to contribute to a dysfunctional lifestyle. We regularly see people who have been trapped in a station of existence over many years: the man who never grows up emotionally and is always like a teenager, a woman who continually struggles with gossip, or people who can't seem to overcome their addictions. I believe what really happens to these people—and many more of us than will admit it—is that we eventually become extremists in our area of dysfunction. In essence, over the years, a person gradually moves to an extreme place in that state of being.

When it comes to judgments, criticism, sarcasm, negativity, complaining, and gossiping, we rarely have these practices in our life in moderation. Each one of these states of being leads to extreme behaviors and lifestyles. The problem with these behaviors is that we are usually living in deception in them and don't recognize the extremity of our behavior. At the same time, there are polar opposites of these lifestyles in the positive realm.

Jesus spoke a very somber statement when He declared there is no middle ground between the kingdom of heaven and the world: "Whoever is not with me is against me, and whoever does not gather with me scatters" (Matt. 12:30, NIV). A person is either with Christ or against Him. There is no middle ground in loving our Lord. You either love Him or are His enemy. A person either works for the kingdom of God or works against it.

And so it is when it comes to judgment, criticism, sarcasm, negativity, complaining, and gossip. They begin small in a person's life and end as extreme negatives with serious consequences. We may think we just gossip a little or complain only now and then or rarely judge others. However, if we are to be authentic followers of Christ, there is little room for these practices in our life: "Those who consider themselves religious and yet do not keep a tight rein on their tongues deceive themselves, and their religion is worthless" (James 1:26, NIV).

THE JUDGE BECOMES CHILDLIKE

> For in the same way you judge others, you will be judged, and with the measure you use, it will be measured to you.
> —MATTHEW 7:2, NIV

Being judgmental is a position in life that guarantees grief and sorrow. A little bit of judgment goes a long way in producing misery. The chronically judgmental person sets in motion one of the eternal laws of the kingdom: you reap what you sow. However, with judgment, you reap so much more than you sow. A judgmental person judges a woman he works with because she is challenged in keeping her weight in check. Later in life, when his wife struggles with a weight problem, he feels the dramatic judgments of others. Or a judgmental person criticizes and judges a friend whose son has a legal issue. When his own son ends up having a legal problem, others harshly judge him as being a failure as a father. Another judgmental person views life through glasses that see only one thing: faults. Because the judgmental person judges everything, others will judge him or her at every turn. To live in the extreme of being judgmental is to bring distress to your own life and those who are near you.

The more childlike we become, though, the less we judge. Being childlike is the farthest extreme position in life from judging. The term *childish* carries a negative connotation that means to be silly or immature, but when we use the term *childlike*, we are representing the purest character qualities of humanity. For example, my four-year-old grandson, Isaac, and I have a standing date every Thursday. We go out to eat at a place where they have a great indoor play area. Isaac always grabs two or three kids, and they play their hearts out. Recently I watched Isaac pick a little boy with Down syndrome and a girl of a difference race to become his playmates. At the end of two hours of playing he cried as we left; he wanted his new, best friends to come home with him. This was so true to the character of a child: simplistic and easy to make happy. The gates of heaven stand open for us, as little children, to enter.

When we become childlike, we accept people for what they are, children of God, made in His image. We do not focus on the imperfection of others in their appearance, words, or actions. To be childlike is to turn from self-seeking ambition, to be free from pride, to be able to forgive and forget, and to be disengaged from the allure of things.

THE CRITIC BECOMES FAITH-FILLED

> By faith he made his home in the promised land like a stranger in a foreign country; he lived in tents, as did Isaac and Jacob, who were heirs with him of the same promise. For he was looking forward to the city with foundations, whose architect and builder is God.
>
> —HEBREWS 11:9–10, NIV

A person who criticizes may end up in the extreme position of a critic or faultfinder. The critic's life is constantly tuned in to what can go wrong. Even when things go right, he or she can find fault. Critical people have no room in life for things to go well. Positive results are not in their paradigm.

A critical person can easily become a cynic and trust no one. Cynics have very few positive relationships. How could they? They believe everyone is selfish and just out for themselves. Cynics have no faith in people or God's power to change circumstances. Cynics are hopeless.

The extreme opposite of being a cynic is being one

who is full of faith and hope in the Lord. This is the land where the Lord wants us to take up permanent residence: the place of faith. The place of faith isn't a physical residence. It doesn't require a 2,500-square-foot house in a gated community with security, and it can be found anywhere in any country. However, the place of faith has one foundation, one architect, and one builder: God.

THE SARCASTIC BECOMES JOY-FILLED

> I have told you this so that my joy may be in you and that your joy may be complete.
>
> —JOHN 15:11, NIV

A person living in the extremes of sarcasm has a soul full of pride. He or she goes around ripping people apart with biting words. Sarcastic people are like buzz saws with words as the blade of the saw. Anyone who gets in their way comes away bleeding emotionally as the sarcastic person's words cut the other person's soul.

Sarcastic people live in unforgiveness. They hurt others with words and leave a trail of wounded people in their lives and don't give it a thought. Living in the extreme of sarcasm leads a person to succumb to a life of bitterness. Bitter people shrivel up emotionally and often physically.

The extreme opposite of sarcasm and bitterness is contentment, a life filled with complete joy. Have you ever been around a person filled with the joy of the Lord? They brighten every room they enter, and their joy is infectious. They find a silver lining in every event in life—good, challenging, and even devastating.

Joy is central to the Christian life. It is a contradiction to say a person is a Christian and not assume he or she has the joy of the Lord. And who couldn't use more joy in their life?

THE PESSIMIST BECOMES OPTIMISTIC

> We know that all things work together for good to those who love God, to those who are called according to His purpose.
>
> —ROMANS 8:28

The extreme life of negativity leads to being mired and engulfed in the past. Everything negative that has ever happened to a person is part of their present experience. The extremely negative person has become the eternal pessimist chained to the past. They have a perpetual outlook on life that anticipates anything that happens will be negative. It is the pessimist who sees life as a glass that is always half-empty. Every positive experience with them has a negative feeling.

The fact is, pessimism is hazardous to your health. Our minds have a direct link to the twelve systems of our bodies—to the nervous system, the endocrine system, the digestive system, and so on. No wonder the pessimist is stressed and nervous! Having created a foundation in his or her life for living chronically ill, he or she is more susceptible to sickness.

Obviously the flip side of being a pessimist is being an optimist. They are at two ends of the continuum.

The optimist sees the silver lining in even the direst of circumstances. The optimist expects the best from people and seems to draw it out of them. The optimist looks at the future and sees all the good that can come to pass. *Optimism* actually comes from the Latin word *optimum,* which means "best."[1]

Optimism has it benefits. People who have an optimistic attitude on life live longer, are depressed less, and are more successful in almost every venue in life, such as work, school, and relationships. Who would you rather be married to, an optimist or a pessimist? Easy answer.

THE COMPLAINER BECOMES GRATEFUL

> I know what it is to be in need, and I know what it is to have plenty. I have learned the secret of being content in any and every situation, whether well fed or hungry, whether living in plenty or in want. I can do all this through him who gives me strength.
>
> —PHILIPPIANS 4:12–13, NIV

The extreme life of complaining parks a person in a territory that is void of the presence of God, and that domain is the land of ingratitude. An ungrateful person can't hear God. God is good, but the ungrateful person can only complain—and complain about everything, even the circumstances and events in life that are good.

The ungrateful person is the emotional counterpart to the physical act of scraping your fingernails down a chalkboard. The continually whining and ungrateful person grates on everyone to the point that people flee their company as fast and they can. Ungrateful people live a life of loneliness. Who wants to be around an ungrateful person? No matter how much you love them and serve them, they can give only one response: ingratitude. And they usually express that ingratitude toward those who sacrifice the most for them.

The thankful person is the counterpart of the complainer. To live in thankfulness or gratitude is to reside in contentment. The Scriptures point to the need for contentment in our lives and link it directly to godliness (1 Tim. 6:6).

The Apostle Paul revealed the secret to living in gratitude and contentment: "Rejoice always. Pray without ceasing. In everything give thanks, for this is the will of God in Christ Jesus concerning you" (1 Thess. 5:16–18). In our prosperous land we have the human propensity to not be grateful for our many blessings, but Paul reminds us the secret to living in gratitude is receiving grace and strength from God for every situation of life.

THE GOSSIP BECOMES TRUSTWORTHY

> A talebearer reveals secrets, but he who is of a faithful spirit conceals the matter.
>
> —PROVERBS 11:13

To gossip is to risk becoming *the* gossip. The gossip is a chief enemy of Christian fellowship. Really? Yes, really. His words do only one thing in the body: cause division. And his words even separate close friends (Prov. 16:28).

The words of a gossip always and on every occasion come against the most essential of all God's purposes for the church—that its members live in unity. Unity and unconditional love for one another is what the Lord knows will draw unsaved people into the kingdom. It is what their lives yearn for and cannot find in the world.

The gossip is described in a number of different ways by the various translations of the Bible, and the descriptions are not very flattering, nor the outcome of gossip edifying. Here are three different translations of Proverbs 16:28:

> A troublemaker plants seeds of strife; gossip separates the best of friends.
>
> —NLT

> A perverse man spreads strife, and a slanderer separates intimate friends.
>
> —NAS

> An evil man provokes judgment and persecutes his friends without cause.
>
> —ABPE

The gossip is a troublemaker, perverse, and an evil person. He separates best, intimate friends and even persecutes his own friends. The extreme opposite of gossip? Absolute, complete, 100 percent confidentiality. How do you rate on the confidentiality scale? Do you keep things 90 percent confidential, 95 percent, or 99 percent? The Lord wants to know He can trust you completely.

My wife and I recently heard a nationally recognized minister say on prime-time television something similar to this: "I've had a lot of well-known people share their stuff with me for prayer and counsel. I've never repeated any of it once to another person." My wife remarked, "Well, now I know why God's blessing him."

LIVE IN THE LIGHT

Christians should be radical extremists when it comes to following Christ and not following the ways of the world. Our declarations should not be words of judgment, criticism, sarcasm, negativity, complaining, or gossip. Our words of declaration should be praise to the Lord, and they should bring encouragement and positive words of life to many. We are meant to live inside God's light:

> But you are a chosen people, a royal priesthood, a holy nation, God's special possession, that you may declare the praises of him who called you out of darkness into his wonderful light.
>
> —1 PETER 2:9, NIV

Part Two

The Forty-Day
Word Fast

Day 1

THE FAST BEGINS

Is not this the kind of fasting I have chosen: to loose the chains of injustice and untie the cords of the yoke, to set the oppressed free and break every yoke?... Then you will call, and the LORD will answer; you will cry for help, and he will say: Here am I. If you do away with the yoke of oppression, with the pointing of the finger and malicious talk...
—ISAIAH 58:6, 9, NIV

Key words: the pointing of the finger and malicious talk

WHAT AN EXCITING challenge! It may be hard for you today to envision changing your habitual judgments of others or the way you size people up when you meet them. I know it was for me when I began working on this area in my life.

So let's start with a preliminary inventory.

During the day do you find yourself being critical of your boss or using sarcastic humor? What is your first response when someone suggests something new—to think about what can go wrong? Do you find yourself complaining about items of little consequence that come along? When was the last time you sat and listened as someone passed on a juicy piece of gossip? When was the last time *you* were the one passing on that little piece of news about another person?

For some, eliminating "the pointing of the finger and malicious talk" will prove to be a lifestyle change in an area that has developed over many years. Or perhaps for you it may be something that already tugs at your heart every time you remember the awful words you can't believe came out of your mouth.

Some things only happen by fasting, and in this case we're referring to fasting words. But such change is possible! And of course we have an intercessor, a great high priest, Christ, standing in the gap for us when we fall short.

The truth is, we can't change our patterns with our words by the arm of the flesh. Galatians 5:17 explains, "For the flesh desires what is contrary to the Spirit, and the Spirit what is contrary to the flesh. They are in conflict with each other, so that you are not to do whatever you want" (NIV). Our flesh doesn't have what it takes to make this kind of change with our words. Bridling this unruly member—the tongue— and bringing it under the control of the Spirit is the greatest of all challenges; however, the Lord has given us the Holy Spirit for just such a purpose.

This is the fast Isaiah chose: a fast to break the bonds of wickedness and the bands of the yoke and to set the oppressed free. By God's grace this is the fast we undertake now—a forty-day fast of words.

Daily Journal

1. What is the Lord speaking to me through these verses today?

   _____

   _____

   _____

2. Were there any particular words that came out of my mouth today I need to repent of? I ask the Holy Spirit to touch my heart and keep these words out of my mouth tomorrow.

   _____

   _____

   _____

3. Where do I most need correction with my words—with judgments, criticism, sarcasm, negativity, complaining, or gossip; or with family, friends, church members, coworkers, acquaintances, authorities, or any others?

   _____

   _____

   _____

Day 2

MEDITATE WELL

Let the words of my mouth and the meditation of my heart be acceptable in Your sight, O Lord, my strength and my Redeemer.
—PSALM 19:14

Key words: let the words of my mouth

CAN YOU HEAR the cry of the psalmist's voice here? It is as though he is saying, "Oh, Lord, that the words coming out of my mouth would be acceptable to You!" What would these kind of words sound like? Clearly not like the words we've been studying here—judgments, criticism, sarcasm, negativity, complaining, or gossip.

What is the best course of action to take to have words that are pleasing to the Lord? One way is to be quiet more, to limit the words coming out of our mouths. We speak so many frivolous words and participate in conversations that are not edifying on any given day. Try this today: in conversations with other people, listen more and speak less. Make your prayer one that says, "Lord, close my mouth."

Closing your mouth will have these immediate effects:

- You won't sin with your words.
- You'll listen more.

- You'll seek to understand, not seek to be understood.
- People will think you're wise.

Is it possible for the Lord to do such a complete work in you that even the meditations of your heart would be acceptable to Him? Yes, it is possible. He tells us in Hebrews that He will save us completely if we come to Him (Heb. 7:25), and when He says completely, He means 100 percent, including each idle word and every thought in our minds. Oh, what a great salvation He has for us!

This is the goal for the word fast—that the Lord would do such a deep work in our hearts that the words that come out of our mouths and the meditations of our hearts would be acceptable to Him.

DAILY JOURNAL

1. What is the Lord speaking to me through these verses today?

_____

_____

_____

2. Were there any particular words that came out of my mouth today I need to repent of?

I ask the Holy Spirit to touch my heart and keep these words out of my mouth tomorrow.

_____

_____

_____

3. What is on my mind most of the time—the thing I think about most—if I'm honest?

_____

_____

_____

Day 3

LORD, GUARD MY LIPS!

Set a guard, O LORD, over my mouth; keep
watch over the door of my lips.
—PSALM 141:3

Key words: set a guard

THIS FORTY-DAY WORD fast isn't about who can be the most disciplined or who can scrutinize their words more thoroughly. It's about setting apart time in the morning to commune with the Lord, being mindful of Him everywhere you go, and putting Him first in everything you do. It's about getting intimate with Jesus in quietness and humility. The fruitfulness we want in our words flows forth from intimacy, since all fruitfulness comes from intimacy with Jesus.

Can you be so intimate with Jesus that He guards your mouth daily? Can we find this kind of life in Jesus? Proverbs 8:34–35 assures us, "Blessed is the man who hears me, watching daily at my gates, waiting at the posts of my doors. For whoever finds me finds life, and will obtain favor of the LORD."

In essence, the psalmist in Psalm 141:3 is praying, "Lord, would You do for me that which I obviously can't do for myself? Guard my mouth and watch over my lips." We have all experienced speaking these words of judgment, criticism, sarcasm, negativity, complaining, and gossip. They escape from our mouths so quickly. They slip past our lips while we're not paying attention. It is only by the Spirit of the Lord that there is hope of bringing our words under the governance of His Spirit.

The forty-day word fast is meant to empty ourselves as much as possible of our own spirit and the words that aren't edifying so that we might take on more of the Holy Spirit and the words He would speak through us. The old has to leave to make room for the new.

Ask yourself this question throughout the day: What words would the Lord have me speak? He will speak to you about this. We will seek the Lord and discover more of this daily during this forty-day fast of words.

DAILY JOURNAL

1. What is the Lord speaking to me through these verses today?

   _____

   _____

   _____

2. Were there any particular words that came
   out of my mouth today I need to repent of?
   I ask the Holy Spirit to touch my heart and
   keep these words out of my mouth tomorrow.

   _____

   _____

   _____

3. How did God help guard my lips today?

   _____

   _____

   _____

Day 4

WHICH KINGDOM RULES?

*O generation of vipers, how can you, being
evil, speak good things? For out of the abundance of the heart the mouth speaks.*
—MATTHEW 12:34

Key words: the mouth speaks

O H, DOES THE mouth speak! Every one of us has
no doubt had that experience, where we spoke and
immediately wished we hadn't spoken. What came out
of our mouth was embarrassing, maybe even hurtful,
to someone else. Perhaps we slipped and said a curse
word or repeated gossip someone told us. Whatever
the case, we wonder, "Where did that come from?"

For me, this truth was driven home when I said
something off-color in front of a couple of ladies in a
coffee shop line. There I was, the leader of a Christian
organization and an elder in my church, and I said
something inappropriate in front of some women I
knew. I was embarrassed the moment the words came
out, but I didn't give it a second thought. I rationalized it wasn't that bad.

A few weeks later, there I was at the same coffee
shop and the exact same comment slipped out in front
of another woman! This time the words grieved me. I

walked away repenting and hearing the Lord tell me there was something wrong with my heart.

Most of us wish we could come up with a different explanation, but the truth is our mouths reveal what is in our hearts. We can make all the excuses:

- "I really didn't mean that."
- "Oh, that just slipped out."
- "That sounded a lot worse than I meant it."
- "They misunderstood what I said."

There can be only one response to the caustic words that come out of our mouths, and that is to recognize those judgments, gossip, or sarcasm as sin and then repent. In this forty-day word fast it is important that you reflect each day on transgressions made with your words. Notice if certain patterns develop. Is there a particular person you are free to gossip with? Are you being critical of your boss or your spouse daily?

The same way a person's language reveals what part of the country he's from or his national origin, as followers of Christ our words quickly reveal what kingdom we're living in. Is it the kingdom of this world or the kingdom of our God? If sarcasm, criticism, and complaining flow forth from our heart to our lips, then our country of origin is exposed as worldly, worldly, and worldly. This forty-day word fast seeks to purify the stream of words that flows from the fountain of our heart.

DAILY JOURNAL

1. What is the Lord speaking to me through these verses today?

_____

_____

_____

2. Were there any particular words that came out of my mouth today I need to repent of? I ask the Holy Spirit to touch my heart and keep these words out of my mouth tomorrow.

_____

_____

_____

3. Have the words I have spoken recently about situations or other people reflected the kingdom of this world or God's kingdom?

_____

_____

_____

Day 5

Use Seasoning Salt

Let your speech always be with grace, seasoned with salt,
that you may know how you should answer everyone.
—Colossians 4:6

Key words: let your speech

WHAT A CHALLENGE this verse presents—to always have your speech full of the grace of the Lord Jesus. It is sobering to think our speech and example may be the only frame of reference another person has for how a Christian speaks and acts. Careless words or actions on our part may bring about in them a lasting prejudice against the gospel of Christ.

So let's consider: What are the first words that come out of your mouth when the waiter serves your order at a restaurant and spills some of the soup on your lap? What about when you splurge and order that rib-eye filet and take the first bite, only to discover it's bloody instead of well done? Are your words seasoned with grace?

As followers of Christ we do not have the freedom to say anything we want, to blurt out whatever is on our mind. We have all heard the excuse, "Well, you know me. I just speak my mind." The Lord has different plans for us. He wants our words to be seasoned with salt. And the salt is grace.

The intention isn't that we constantly talk about the grace of our Lord with people we meet. He wants us to use wisdom in what we say and yet give testimony to His saving grace when the opportune occasions arise. Paul encourages us in this key verse in Colossians to always have our speech be filled with grace. Do we show the grace of God in our words toward others?

Through the deep work of the Holy Spirit in our lives during this forty-day word fast we can always expect to have a gracious word for each person we encounter. Instead of negative words, sarcasm, or words that bring people down, the Lord's grace can season our speech. The Lord's grace operating in our lives enables us to know how to respond to every person we meet with words of encouragement and life. It is possible. Almost every one of us know a gracious person; they are gentle, humble, and not overbearing. We are drawn to them.

Let us commit this day to speak words of love, charity, encouragement, and kindness.

DAILY JOURNAL

1. What is the Lord speaking to me through these verses today?

_____

_____

_____

2. Were there any particular words that came out of my mouth today I need to repent of? I ask the Holy Spirit to touch my heart and keep these words out of my mouth tomorrow.

_____

_____

_____

3. In what ways did I use words that weren't seasoned with grace today?

_____

_____

_____

4. Did I use words that weren't seasoned with grace today? If so, when?

_____

_____

_____

Day 6

HEARING AND SPEAKING GOD'S WORDS

The Sovereign LORD has given me a well-instructed
tongue, to know the word that sustains the weary.
He wakens me morning by morning, wakens
my ear to listen like one being instructed.
—ISAIAH 50:4, NIV

Key words: to know the word that
sustains the weary

IN THIS PROPHETIC snapshot of Jesus in Isaiah, the Holy Spirit was upon Him so He could speak words that encouraged and sustained those in need. This image shows Jesus as a disciple being awakened every morning by God the Father. And Jesus has an ear to hear. That concept of having an ear to hear—one that understands the words the Spirit is saying—is used repeatedly throughout the Scriptures, in particular in the Book of Revelation: "He who has an ear, let him hear what the Spirit says to the churches" (Rev. 2:17; 3:6, 22).

Jesus went to be with the Father so that we might have the Holy Spirit available to us. Through His power, we can rid our lives of these negative words that have been engrained in our speech patterns by the world, our upbringing, and our experiences. We can begin to speak a new language, the language of heaven. The kingdom of heaven is within us—in our midst, as Luke 17:20–21 teaches—and we can be awakened every morning to listen to the Holy Spirit's instruction. The twofold promise of God to us is that we can have a tongue that speaks words that sustain others, and we can have ears to hear God's words to us. If we want to speak His words, we first need to be quiet and listen to what He is saying.

Every day we see weary, hurting people. Hurting people are wounded easily by words. They harm others with their words, and they injure themselves with the words they speak. Remember to not take hurting people's words personally.

The Lord has called us to give words of encouragement, grace, and life to these hurting people. We must be cognizant of every person the Lord brings across our paths—not just the lovely, but also the unlovely; not just the popular, but also the unpopular; not just the successful, but also the weary. Rees Howell said it this way: "I started at the bottom and loved just one; and if you love one, you can love many; and if many, you can love all."[1]

Cry out to the Lord for the tongue of a disciple every morning so that you can empty yourself of words of judgment, criticism, sarcasm, negative words, complaining, and gossip, and instead be filled with His words. It only takes a single word, the right Spirit-filled word, to sustain the weary. He can give us the words to speak, the right word at the right time, a word spoken in due season.

Daily Journal

1. What is the Lord speaking to me through these verses today?

_____

_____

_____

2. Were there any particular words that came out of my mouth today that I need to repent of? I ask the Holy Spirit to touch my heart and keep these words out of my mouth tomorrow.

_____

_____

_____

3. Who are the hurting and weary people crossing my path right now? What words might the Holy Spirit be giving me to speak to them?

_____

_____

_____

LIFE OR DEATH—YOU CHOOSE

Death and life are in the power of the tongue,
and those who love it will eat its fruit.
—**PROVERBS 18:21**

Key words: death and life are in the
power

T HE WORDS THAT cross our tongues have incredible power. They bring encouragement or discouragement, blessings or curses, praise or criticism, healing or injury, clarity or confusion, inspiration or depression. Gentle words have the power to soothe the soul of those in distress. Criticism can paralyze the most positive of persons. The elevating and destructive power of our words is both awesome and sobering.

Each one of us yearns to hear motivating words of praise. When it comes to praise, most of us are like little children whose faces light up when they are praised or applauded. Few of us can tolerate the critical eye of an acquaintance or employer who always looks for the error and seldom acknowledges the positive. Given the opportunity to not interact with a negative person or complainer, we will exit the scene quickly.

Have you ever had an outstanding boss or employer? Some bosses can inspire and motivate, but many others fail miserably in getting their employees to fully

117

engage in their responsibilities. Why do some supervisors run effective, positive teams and others seem to fall flat in motivating their charges?

In thirty-plus years of managing people I've concluded that effectiveness is driven by communication—the right kind of communication. Sure, leaders have to express goals, have regular meetings, develop their people, and give feedback. However, we leaders need to liberally give praise, encouragement, or recognition for a job well done. This kind of feedback seems to motivate almost anyone. On the flip side we need to be very cautious to not use the words that produce discouragement and a negative workplace, including criticism without instruction, putdowns, sarcastic comments, judgments, and other negative words.

My personal mantra is to tell people when they hit or miss the mark and what they need to work on to be successful, but I want be sure to praise them more than I critique. Any time I lead meetings, whether it is with a few or hundreds, I always start with an "atta boy" or "atta girl." My goal: to praise and recognize achievement, faithfulness, hard work, and those who show kindness and compassion to others. I ask employees to send me names of people who are doing the things mentioned above, and then I recognize them accordingly in meetings, newsletters, and communication pieces.

Where do you have the occasion to give life or death with your words? Is it as a father or mother, disciple maker, employee or employer, or husband or wife? Few practices can benefit a relationship more or turn it around faster than becoming a person who praises rather than criticizes or is negative. And remember, those negative words have dramatically more impact than positive words.

DAILY JOURNAL

1. What is the Lord speaking to me through these verses today?

_____

_____

_____

2. Were there any particular words that came out of my mouth today that I need to repent of? I ask the Holy Spirit to touch my heart and keep these words out of my mouth tomorrow.

_____

_____

_____

3. How have my words delivered life today? How have they delivered death?

_____

_____

_____

Day 8

WORDS OF PRAISE

I will bless the LORD at all times; His praise
will continually be in my mouth.
—PSALM 34:1

Key words: His praise will continually be in my mouth.

MY CLOSEST FRIEND, Ben, is on a quest to discover the Lord's wisdom in his life. This particular man is a worshipper—oh, how he can worship! And as Ben and I started our forty-day word fast together, he helped me connect the dots between the wisdom of God and our worship and the fear of the Lord.

It was just a matter of days into our fast before we asked, "What words *should* be in our mouths instead of judgment, criticism, sarcasm, negativity, complaints, and gossip?" Ben's first thought was that the answer was wisdom—that the Lord wants words of wisdom coming from our mouths instead of these other negative words. Immediately we connected the dots to the proverb that says the fear of the Lord is the beginning of wisdom (Prov. 9:10).

What does the fear of the Lord mean? One aspect is the awe we encounter when we come to know the Lord as our Savior. When I reflect on my struggles in life, from pornography to self-centeredness, my sins seem unforgivable and overwhelming. It is beyond humbling to think He took all my sins and the sins of all humanity on Himself. Then I understand the Lord's awesome holiness. He was tempted in every way as a man yet was without sin. He was completely, perfectly sinless. Such awe and fear at the Lord's perfection turns to worship and praise as I catch a glimpse of the Lord's holiness. He is holy, holy, holy. Oh, how awesome is the Lord, worthy to be praised! The blood of the Lamb has washed my shame and my sin away— and He's done the same for you.

What, then, should be on our lips instead of judgment, criticism, sarcasm, negativity, complaints, and gossip? Words of praise and thanksgiving.

DAILY JOURNAL

1. What is the Lord speaking to me through these verses today?

   _____

   _____

   _____

2. Were there any particular words that came out of my mouth today that I need to repent of? I ask the Holy Spirit to touch my heart

and keep these words out of my mouth
tomorrow.

_____

_____

_____

3. How am I growing in worship and praise of
   the Lord?

_____

_____

_____

Day 9

DON'T BE RECKLESS

The words of the reckless pierce like swords, but the tongue of the wise brings healing.
—**PROVERBS 12:18**, NIV

Key words: the words of the reckless pierce like swords

OH, TO TAKE back some of the sarcastic, judgmental words I have said in the past! Maybe you can relate. But it simply isn't that easy. If we have slandered someone, repeated gossip, judged someone, or made cutting sarcastic comments, we need to recognize those words for what they are: sin that requires repentance and the seeking of forgiveness.

The Lord forgives; others may not. Reconciliation takes two people. Our gossip and judgments may do serious harm to someone and their reputation. Even if they forgive us, the residue of the damage remains. That damage will take a long time to fade away or be made right. Negative words—especially criticism, judgment, and gossip—also cause collateral damage. When others hear these damaging words, they're influenced in a negative way. They're also hurt by our negative words about their friends and loved ones. Negative words travel far and fast.

Sarcasm, complaining, and negative words have

been a deep part of my life at times. I have been very sarcastic and critical during different seasons. As I became sensitized to my words during this fast, I more quickly recognized and repented of my sinful words when they came out. For instance, one time on the way to church I made a very sarcastic comment to my wife. Later in the day I brought it up and asked her to forgive me. She remarked, "I didn't notice it. It's such a natural part of your life and conversations." I told her right there and then, "The Lord is working in my life, and this is going to change."

Does it need to change in your life too?

Notice the word *reckless* in today's verse. Words are so powerful and yet used recklessly by so many. Our caustic words can resemble a person carrying around a razor-sharp, double-edged sword thrust in the air, cutting people indiscriminately. Contrast this wholesale wounding of others to the tongue of a wise person described in the second half of today's proverb: "But the tongue of the wise brings healing." What do those healing words look like? They are gentle, encouraging, full of appropriate praise, and gracious. They are spoken in due season, at just the right moment.

My personal experience is that the further we go into this forty-day word fast, the more sensitive we become toward negative words—in particular those coming out of our own mouths. Let me encourage you to pray that the Lord give you the strength and wisdom to seek forgiveness from those you harm with your words and to forgive those who harm you with theirs.

DAILY JOURNAL

1. What is the Lord speaking to me through these verses today?

_____

_____

_____

2. Were there any particular words that came out of my mouth today that I need to repent of. I ask the Holy Spirit to touch my heart and keep these words out of my mouth tomorrow.

_____

_____

_____

3. Is there anyone I've offended with my words whose forgiveness I need to seek?

_____

_____

_____

Day 10

THE SNARE OF GOSSIP

*A perverse person stirs up conflict, and
a gossip separates close friends.*
—PROVERBS 16:28, NIV

Key words: separates close friends

MOST OF US have been hurt by gossip at one time or another. Gossip is destructive and difficult to control. In most instances it seems as if we are defenseless against its spread.

If you have felt the personal sting of gossip, then you probably remember the sorrowful, deep, cutting pain of it. If you dwell too long on a particular incident, it might bring tears to your eyes. And as if the wounds in your soul aren't sufficiently damaging enough, there's also the separation that comes when friends or loved ones are involved. Gossip has the potential to change relationships for a lifetime. Of all the challenges in living the Christian life, forgiving those who participated in gossip about you ranks near the top. The only remedy to the damage done from gossip is the gift of forgiveness that comes only from the Lord.

Time after time you see people separated because of someone breaking a confidence by sharing information, spreading a rumor, or purposefully repeating a matter to harm someone. When we hear something about someone, we should not share that information with anyone else that is not part of the problem or part of the solution to the problem. Scripture tells us we should treat others with the same courtesy with which we would like to be treated—"Therefore, everything you would like men to do to you, do also to them, for this is the Law and the Prophets" (Matt. 7:12).

One element of gossip that is subtle in its entrapment and must be guarded against is the gossip that can happen through prayer. Christians often couch their gossip as prayer requests, asking for or sharing intimate details so people might "pray more effectively." This is nonsense, because God knows the details of every situation and doesn't need us reminding Him of every little element. While it sounds pious, this kind of talk among Christians is just as destructive as gossiping over coffee in the break room.

When we contemplate the ways we can express our love for one another, we think in lofty terms—in terms of sacrifice, lavish giving, or other grandiose acts. Covering another person's sin and not participating in gossip is challenging, courageous, and exhibits a depth of love to which we all aspire. In this we show our deep love and preference for one another.

DAILY JOURNAL

1. What is the Lord speaking to me through
   these verses?

   _____

   _____

   _____

2. Were there any particular words that came
   out of my mouth today that I need to repent
   of? I ask the Holy Spirit to touch my heart
   and keep these words out of my mouth
   tomorrow.

   _____

   _____

   _____

3. Where do I stand in my forgiveness of others
   who have gossiped about me? Where might
   I need to seek forgiveness from those I have
   gossiped about?

   _____

   _____

   _____

AN ENCOUNTER WITH THE HOLY

And I said: "Woe is me! For I am undone because I am a man of unclean lips, and I dwell in the midst of a people of unclean lips. For my eyes have seen the King, the LORD of Hosts." Then one of the seraphim flew to me with a live coal which he had taken with the tongs from off the altar in his hand. And he laid it on my mouth, and said, "This has touched your lips, and your iniquity is taken away, and your sin purged."
—ISAIAH 6:5–7

Key words: And he laid it on my mouth, and said, "This has touched your lips, and your iniquity is taken away, and your sin purged."

IN TODAY'S PASSAGE we see Isaiah having an encounter with God. He saw God! He also saw the seraphim, which was an angel of the highest order associated with purity. Numerous other men had encounters with God in the Scriptures, and their responses were different but similar:

- Moses: "At this, Moses hid his face, because he was afraid to look at God" (Exod. 3:6, NIV).

- Ezekiel: "This was the appearance of the likeness of the glory of the LORD. When I saw it, I fell facedown, and I heard the voice of one speaking" (Ezek. 1:28, NIV).

- Job: "My ears had heard of you but now my eyes have seen you. Therefore I despise myself and repent in dust and ashes" (Job 42:5–6, NIV).

- John the disciple: "When I saw him, I fell at his feet as though dead" (Rev. 1:17, NIV).

- Peter, upon realizing who Jesus was: "He fell at Jesus' knees and said, 'Go away from me, Lord; I am a sinful man!'" (Luke 5:8, NIV).

Though each of these men had their own unique response, they also had one similar reaction: a look at themselves compared to the Lord. They fell facedown, were afraid, were as dead, and despised themselves and repented. Upon seeing God, they saw their sinfulness.

When Isaiah heard the seraphim calling out, "Holy, holy, holy," his immediate thought was to reflect and realize he was defiled by the words that had come out of his mouth, across his lips—the sin of his words. He heard the seraphim's words and came face-to-face with his own words. He was caught short.

We too are defiled by the words that come out of our mouths. And there is only one who can cleanse us and forgive our sins: Christ, our Savior. He can speak a word and make us clean: "You are already clean through the word which I have spoken to you"

(John 15:3). His Spirit gives us the power to release clean words from our lips.

There is a pivotal lesson in these scriptures of Isaiah that we can't afford to miss. We must recognize the sin of our words and repent, knowing the Lord has forgiveness for us. Then there is a further step Isaiah took that the Lord beckons each of us to take. He says, "Also I heard the voice of the Lord saying, 'Whom shall I send, and who will go for us?' Then I said, 'Here am I. Send me'" (Isa. 6:8).

As the Lord cleanses our lives of the negative, destructive words of our mouths, will we answer His call? Will we allow His words to cross our lips and give words of life to others? Thank you, Lord Jesus, for cleansing us and giving us the power to speak words of life to others!

DAILY JOURNAL

1. What is the Lord speaking to me through these verses?

_____

_____

_____

2. Were there any particular words that came out of my mouth today that I need to repent of? I ask the Holy Spirit to touch my heart

and keep these words out of my mouth tomorrow.

_____

_____

_____

3. What is your response to encountering the holiness of God?

_____

_____

_____

Day 12

WISE OR FOOLISH?

*A fool's mouth lashes out with pride, but
the lips of the wise protect them.*
—PROVERBS 14:3, NIV

Key words: but the lips of the wise
protect them

CONTRAST A FOOL'S mouth and the lips of the wise. The fool's mouth makes him vulnerable; the wise person's lips protect him. The proud, foolish person doesn't understand the ramifications of his words, lashing out in pride and saying whatever he wants; the wise person understands the power of words and is protected because he weighs the words that cross his lips. The fool's words inflict wounds on others, and his words eventually injure him; the wise person's words deliver life to others, and his words protect him from wounding.

Let's compare the two.

The Fool's Words	The Wise Person's Words
Harm others	Bring life to others
Harm himself	Protect him
Full of pride	Humble
Spoken rashly	Spoken with care
Cause him punishment	Bring him honor

Wisdom is a key to life and peace. With wisdom comes great safety—and there is so much to be protected from in this out-of-control culture. Wisdom guides us in the choice of our words and teaches us to be peaceful, humble, and gentle with them. With pride, however, comes much confusion in life. The proud person is susceptible to the evils of our society. The proud person's words are harsh and cutting.

It is a viscous circle. Pride causes us to act foolishly and to consider our words more important than other people's. We speak out rashly and suffer the consequences. We expose our ignorance. We are all ignorant about something. We just don't know it all, unless we are full of pride and self-deceit.

We are our own worst enemy in life when we speak in pride. But godly wisdom positions us to receive all the benefits Christ offers us as His followers. Where does godly wisdom begin? It has its roots in the fear of the Lord that produces meekness (humility).

James gives us a wonderful description of godly wisdom in action.

> Who is wise and understanding among you? Let him show his works by his good life in the meekness of wisdom. But if you have bitter envying and strife in your hearts, do not boast and do not lie against the truth. This wisdom descends not from above, but is earthly, unspiritual, and devilish. For where there is envying and strife, there is confusion and every evil work. But the wisdom that is from above is first pure, then peaceable, gentle, open to

reason, full of mercy and good fruits, without partiality, and without hypocrisy. And the fruit of righteousness is sown in peace by those who make peace.

—James 3:13–18

Godly wisdom is shown by how you treat people and the words you speak to them, words of life or death. Godly wisdom is not all about what you know. Oh, Lord, give us wisdom in our use of words!

DAILY JOURNAL

1. What is the Lord speaking to me through these verses?

_____

_____

_____

2. Were there any particular words that came out of my mouth today that I need to repent of? I ask the Holy Spirit to touch my heart and keep these words out of my mouth tomorrow.

_____

_____

_____

3. How do my words reflect wisdom or foolishness as I communicate, in person as well as through social media, texts, and e-mail?

_____

_____

_____

Day 13

What Comes First?

Give ear to my words, O LORD; consider my medita-
tion. Listen to the voice of my cry, my King and my
God, for to You will I pray. O LORD, in the morning
You will hear my voice; in the morning I will direct
my prayer to You, and I will watch expectantly.
—PSALM 5:1–3

Key words: in the morning

THERE IS NO more fruitful way to start the day than to cry out to the Lord. Our days are so busy. There is so much to do and so many important things to accomplish. Let the first words on our lips each day be, "I need you, my Lord and Savior, my rock."

Our Savior made it His practice to steal away early in the morning hours to meet the Father in quietness and personal devotion. (See Mark 1:35 and Luke 5:16.) It made no difference that He was up late the night before ministering to the needs of others. He started the day out in a solitary place with the Father. Often the disciples would be frantically searching for Him in the morning, and He would be gone to a quiet place in the mountains.

Jesus had much to do. As His ministry gained momentum, thousands of people followed after Him, even running after Him. He was concerned about the provision for such crowds. It is estimated that the crowd of men, women, and children surrounding Him when the miracle of the loaves and fishes took place could have been as high as ten thousand.[1] He faced tremendous pressure. The pressures were so great and He had so much to do that He desperately needed this time with His Father. The first words out of His mouth each day were words of intimacy with the Father.

If Jesus needed to direct His first words each day toward His Father in heaven, how much more do we need to reserve the first words out of our mouths for Him each day too—words of adoration, confession, thanksgiving, and prayer. If we are going to cleanse the world's words from our hearts and mouths, we must meet our Jesus anew every day.

DAILY JOURNAL

1. What is the Lord speaking to me through these verses?

_____

_____

_____

2. Were there any particular words that came out of my mouth today that I need to repent of? I ask the Holy Spirit to touch my heart

and keep these words out of my mouth
tomorrow.

_____

_____

_____

3. What do my early morning hours with God
look like?

_____

_____

_____

Day 14

BEHIND ENEMY LINES

Bless those who persecute you; bless and do not curse.
—ROMANS 12:14

Key word: bless

HAVE YOU EVER had a true enemy? A true enemy is out to destroy you. He doesn't want you to just fail; he wants you devastated. He doesn't want you embarrassed; he wants you humiliated. He doesn't want to harm you alone; he wants to wound your family. There are no depths to which he will not plunge to attack you. He will have you covertly watched and your phone conversations recorded. He will put all of his financial resources into seeing you decimated.

I have had such an enemy, and I can tell you this: Once you experience a true enemy, you understand how even in the experience of persecution, the Lord does not want negative words to come forth from your mouth. How scandalous! Can you imagine being so refined through the fire that you respond to persecution with words that bless those persecuting you? But with Him all things are possible.

God will give us the grace needed to bless those who persecute us or purposely try to hurt us. However, we must see persecution from God's perspective. He is concerned about us finding our life in Him and becoming mature disciples. We are concerned with results and outcomes, success and failure, production and output. He is concerned with the depth of our life in Him and with faithfulness. Perhaps it is only through suffering, pain, or persecution that we are able to sift through the frivolities of life, discarding those things that have no eternal significance.

Gene Edwards begins his book *The Prison in the Third Cell* with these words: "It has been said that it is impossible to forgive a man who deliberately hurts you for the sole purpose of destroying you or lowering you. If this be true, you have but one hope: to see this unfair hurt as coming by permission from God for the purpose of lifting your stature above that place where formerly you stood."[1]

If we can see persecution as God lifting our stature above a place from a place where we formerly stood, then we will be able to say as Joseph, "But as for you, you intended to harm me, but God intended it for good, in order to bring it about as it is this day, to save many lives" (Gen. 50:20). God is calling us up to a higher level of faith, a higher level of obedience, and a higher level of trust. He can use persecution to thrust us into the fullness of faith and trust that He desires to establish in us.

DAILY JOURNAL

1. What is the Lord speaking to me through
   these verses?

   _____

   _____

   _____

2. Were there any particular words that came
   out of my mouth today that I need to repent
   of? I ask the Holy Spirit to touch my heart
   and keep these words out of my mouth
   tomorrow.

   _____

   _____

   _____

3. How can I purpose in my heart to bless
   those who have tried to harm me?

   _____

   _____

   _____

SET A GUARD

Whoever guards his mouth and his tongue
keeps his soul from trouble.
—**PROVERBS 21:23**

Key words: guards his mouth and
his tongue

GUARDING THE MOUTH. Only speaking truth, and without any guile. Injuring no man, and not provoking others. Having the conscience clear, being free from quarrels, contentions, and lawsuits. Guarding the mind, emotions, and will. How many times I wish my lifestyle had mirrored the words written here and that I had walked in this kind of wisdom!

There will be times in life that it doesn't make sense in the natural to guard our words. Our culture encourages us to speak words that justify—to defend ourselves with words, and then get even if need be; to sell ourselves to others with flowery words if we want promotion of some kind; to look out for ourselves because no one else will. Yet God's Word says that if we walk in wisdom and guard our mouths, our lives will be free from calamity. We must line up our lives with the Word of God. Scripture says, "My son, let them not depart from your eyes—keep sound wisdom and discretion; so they will be life to your soul and grace to your neck. Then you will walk safely in your way, and your foot will not stumble" (Prov. 3:21-23).

This forty-day word fast is intended to teach us to guard our words. Let me remind you that the word *fast* means "to cover the mouth." We show great wisdom by simply covering our mouths and not speaking. When we cover our mouths and do not speak injurious words, we save ourselves from pain, suffering, misunderstandings, and all manner of evils that are caused by judgments, criticism, sarcasm, complaints, and gossip.

We have learned from scripture that we can't change our hearts; only the Lord can do that. However, He does give us the directive to *guard* our hearts. The injurious words we speak come directly from the heart and over the tongue. The only way we can avoid speaking these negative words is by guarding our mouths and what comes out of them. Pray for strength today to cover your mouth.

DAILY JOURNAL

1. What is the Lord speaking to me through these verses?

   _____

   _____

   _____

2. Were there any particular words that came out of my mouth today that I need to repent

of? I ask the Holy Spirit to touch my heart and keep these words out of my mouth tomorrow.

_____

_____

_____

3. What words come out of my mouth in more unguarded moments—such as while I am driving?

_____

_____

_____

Day 16

SPEECH 101

Sin is not ended by multiplying words, but the prudent hold their tongues.
—PROVERBS 10:19, NIV

Key words: by multiplying words

IT IS JUST best sometimes to be silent. As Rumi, the thirteenth-century philosopher and poet, said, "Silence is the language of God, all else is poor translation."[1]

Let's think about this in a couple different ways.

First, the more we talk, the greater the risk of offense, misunderstanding, and confusion. In other words, the more you talk, the greater chance you have to get in trouble by something you say. What is the normal reaction when we find ourselves in a troubling situation brought on by something we said? We try to talk our way out of it. This verse in Proverbs is so true in this way: we think we can talk our way out of just about anything we are caught doing wrong. We think, "If I could explain just a little more," or, "If I could just clarify what I really meant." What should we do then? Just hold our tongues; repent where it is necessary; then, be quiet.

Second, consider our model, Jesus. The Sermon on the Mount, spanning three chapters in the Book of Matthew, is approximately two thousand words long. If

Jesus spoke the sermon at a slow rate of 100 words per minute, it would have taken Him twenty minutes to deliver it. Actually it takes only about eighteen minutes to speak the sermon at a normal rate, as the average person speaks 110–115 words per minute. Remember that the next time you are asked to speak somewhere! I always had a personal rule to never speak more than twenty minutes. If Jesus took twenty minutes for the Sermon on the Mount, what do I have to say that is so important it should take longer than that?

And third, when it comes to prayer, we just don't need a ton of words. I discovered that when I got serious about prayer, I ran out of words when trying to speak to the Lord. There is no use or reason to try to impress the Lord with eloquent words.

There are just very few situations in life where an abundance of flamboyant words does the trick. And, yes, it does take great restraint sometimes to not speak. However, when in doubt, don't speak.

Jesus promises to be our personal speech coach through the Holy Spirit. The Bible tells us, "But the Counselor, the Holy Spirit, whom the Father will send in My name, will teach you everything and remind you of all that I told you" (John 14:26). We have access to the same promise Moses received when the Lord said to him in Exodus, "Now therefore go, and I will be with your mouth and teach you what you must say" (Exod. 4:12). Yes, He will even give us the words to speak! Granted, they may not be overwhelming in number or impressive in sophistication, but at least we will never be accused of being a sesquipedalian—one characterized by trying to use long words to impress. (Oops, sorry about that!)

DAILY JOURNAL

1. What is the Lord speaking to me through these verses?

_____

_____

_____

2. Were there any particular words that came out of my mouth today that I need to repent of? I ask the Holy Spirit to touch my heart and keep these words out of my mouth tomorrow.

_____

_____

_____

3. How did I use constraint today in my conversations with others?

_____

_____

_____

KEEP IT COVERED

Brothers and sisters, do not slander one another. Anyone
who speaks against a brother or sister or judges them speaks
against the law and judges it. When you judge the law,
you are not keeping it, but sitting in judgment on it.
—JAMES 4:11, NIV

Key words: do not slander one
another

WHEN WE JUDGE, belittle, condemn, curse, spread rumors, or repeat the failures and sins of other believers, we are just like the world. There are few actions more common to this world than speaking against someone or judging their actions, their motives, how they spend their money, how they look, what kind of car they drive, or how their kids behave. The judgments with which people assault one another are unending.

But it should not be this way among Christians. In this scripture James echoes the words of Jesus: "Judge not, that you be not judged" (Matt. 7:1). As common as the action of judging people is in the world, this action is foreign to the true spirit of Christian fellowship with one another. The scripture is explicit; there is a different standard that we must follow as Christians when it comes to the way we speak about another believer.

In particular love demands that we not uncover the sins of a believer to others. Remember there is a great difference between *covering up* and *uncovering*. Covering up implies keeping something secret from coming to the light that should be brought out in the open. Perhaps someone has broken the law or not followed required policies in a business or organization. You may have had the experience of being pressured by a brother or sister in the Lord to not expose their sin when in reality you had a responsibility to let the proper people know the deceit at hand. If we are keeping something hidden from the people who should know it, then we are wrong and covering up. This does not honor the Lord.

However, we uncover another Christian when we speak about that person's sins or failures to someone else for no good reason. Scripture admonishes us that we not speak about a person's sins to anyone else. Remember 1 Peter 4:8: "Above all, love each other deeply, because love covers over a multitude of sins" (NIV).

DAILY JOURNAL

1. What is the Lord speaking to me through these verses?

_____

_____

_____

2. Were there any particular words that came out of my mouth today that I need to repent of? I ask the Holy Spirit to touch my heart and keep these words out of my mouth tomorrow.

_____

_____

_____

3. How am I choosing not to uncover the sins of my brothers and sisters in Christ? In what ways do I need to work on this?

_____

_____

_____

Day 18

THE WORDS OF THE WORLD

But among you there must not be even a hint of sexual
immorality, or of any kind of impurity, or of greed,
because these are improper for God's holy people. Nor
should there be obscenity, foolish talk or coarse joking,
which are out of place, but rather thanksgiving.
—EPHESIANS 5:3–4, NIV

Key words: nor should there be obscenity, foolish talk or coarse joking

---

WE LIVE IN a toxic, verbal culture. The words people speak in normal conversations have become blatantly filthy and obscene. The filthiness of the language in our society has reached an all-time extreme with the use of obscenities in everyday language. But the Word of God speaks directly to what has happened in the culture of communication in our nation. There is no guessing where it stands on filthy communication. There should be none of it in a follower of Christ. In today's scripture Paul instructs the followers of Christ at Ephesus that this kind of obscene, foolish talk, or coarse joking is improper and out of place for those who follow Christ.

Paul gives explicit direction about the words that come out of our mouths in the above passage. There are to be no obscene words that pass from our lips—nothing that relates to shameful or indecent talk that refers to the sins of the flesh. Talking about sins of the flesh is one of many obscene areas of conversation that seems to be a normal part of the dialogue you hear today. Whether on the TV or in movies, immoral, sexual subjects are spoken about in a matter-of-fact manner.

Foolish talk should be something in which we choose not to participate. The foolish talk referenced here is talk that has no benefit to anyone. No one is being taught the things of the Lord; no one is being encouraged; no one is being profited in any manner. The conversation is just senseless babble. All of us would do well to reflect on Christ's words in Matthew 12:36: "But I say to you that for every idle word that men speak, they will give an account on the Day of Judgment." Now there is a sobering statement!

It is revealing to look deeply into what Paul was communicating about jesting. Jesting is simply speaking in a joking manner. It is a form of humor, and there is nothing intrinsically wrong with jesting. However, Paul was speaking directly to *coarse* jesting, jesting that in its roughness hurts others and causes harm. Paul draws the line in the sand. Coarse jesting is to have no part in a Christian's use of humor.

To complete the instruction on words of obscenity, foolish talk, and coarse jesting, Paul instructs us on what words *should* come out of our mouths. He simply says thanksgiving. The polar opposite could not be more distinct in his comparison. Instead of these negative, filthy, hurtful words, Paul wants us to express to God our thanksgiving. Yes, thanksgiving—the language of heaven.

DAILY JOURNAL

1. What is the Lord speaking to me through these verses?

_____

_____

_____

2. Were there any particular words that came out of my mouth today that I need to repent of? I ask the Holy Spirit to touch my heart and keep these words out of my mouth tomorrow.

_____

_____

_____

3. Where does obscenity, foolish talk, or coarse jesting show up in my words?

_____

_____

_____

Day 19

Post a Watch

Those who guard their lips preserve their lives, but
those who speak rashly will come to ruin.
—**Proverbs 13:3, niv**

Key words: Those who guard their
lips preserve their lives

HAVE YOU EVER known people who take pride in speaking their minds? They don't care who they hurt. They let the chips fall where they may. They leave a wake of destruction in their paths wherever they go. Sometimes these people will go so as far as to proclaim they are speaking the truth of the Lord that needs to be said. After all, if they don't say it, who will? They can't seem to comprehend that truth and grace are different sides of the same coin; they complement each other: "For the law was given through Moses; grace and truth came through Jesus Christ" (John 1:17).

Keeping watch over our words can preserve our lives. The Hebrew meaning for *guard* in Proverbs 13:3 is to keep watch.[1] It is the same word used in Proverbs 4:23, which says, "Above all else, guard your heart, for everything you do flows from it" (NIV). It implies standing watch as a military soldier at the gate of the city. The city is kept safe as long as the soldier keeps constant guard. It is the same way with our lives; it is preserved by watching our words and thinking thoroughly before speaking. The antitheses is opening our mouths wide and speaking whatever comes to mind; therein lies ruin and great injury to many, in particular to ourselves.

When we think before we speak, we suppress evil in our lives, even if we had the thoughts in our minds that we shouldn't speak. By not blurting out words before thinking, we keep our souls from a great deal of guilt and grief. True, we must give account to the Lord for our thoughts; however, there is so much less damage done if we don't speak those thoughts aloud and hurt others.

Let's stand guard diligently over the words coming out of our mouths. And let's dedicate our words to build up and comfort others, to spur others on to pursue the Lord.

DAILY JOURNAL

1. What is the Lord speaking to me through these verses?

   _____

   _____

   _____

2. Were there any particular words that came out of my mouth today that I need to repent of? I ask the Holy Spirit to touch my heart

and keep these words out of my mouth
tomorrow.

_____

_____

_____

3. How did I stand guard over the words of my
   mouth today?

_____

_____

_____

Day 20

FIND THE SECRET PLACE

*By faith we understand that the universe was framed
by the word of God, so that things that are seen
were not made out of things which are visible.*
—HEBREWS 11:3

Key words: by the word of God

T HE WORLD WAS not made out of things you can
see. You can't see spoken words nor can you see faith
with the physical eye. The words God spoke framed
the universe and set it in motion, and it stands today
in obedience to His words.

The Word of God controls the spirit world.
Conversely the natural world is controlled by the
spoken word. Our challenge is to choose our words
carefully and to so abide in Christ that we hear and
speak His words. The same God who spoke to Moses
speaks to us. When we speak His words, we speak
words of life and healing to those around us. His
words are living, active, and sharper than a two-edged
sword, able to judge the thoughts and intentions of
the heart (Heb. 4:12). His words are full of power and
might. By His words, destinies are realized, dreams
fulfilled, and inheritances claimed.

When we find the secret place of abiding in Christ,
we submit our entire souls and spirits to Him—every

thought, word, emotion, and action. It is in the secret place that fruitfulness comes forth in our lives, in our actions, and in the words we speak. Remember, all fruitfulness comes from the intimacy of relationship with Jesus, abiding in Him, for He says, "I am the vine, you are the branches. He who remains in Me, and I in him, bears much fruit. For without Me you can do nothing....My Father is glorified by this, that you bear much fruit; so you will be My disciples" (John 15:5, 8).

As we continually live in the secret place, His words become our words. In Him let us live and move and have our being.

DAILY JOURNAL

1. What is the Lord speaking to me through these verses?

   _____

   _____

   _____

2. Were there any particular words that came out of my mouth today that I need to repent of? I ask the Holy Spirit to touch my heart and keep these words out of my mouth tomorrow.

   _____

   _____

   _____

3. How am I in touch with the secret, invisible
   words of God?

   _____

   _____

   _____

RESTRAIN YOUR SPEECH

The one who has knowledge uses words with restraint, and whoever has understanding is even-tempered. Even fools are thought wise if they keep silent, and discerning if they hold their tongues.
—**PROVERBS 17:27–28,** NIV

Key words: the one who has knowledge uses words with restraint

---

MOST OF US have been around someone who has an opinion about everything. Perhaps we have been that person at some point. We might call that person opinionated; however, the scripture calls him foolish.

How much more prudent it is to be a person who is careful when he speaks and speaks with purpose, having something to say. We have all had the experience of putting our foot in our mouth by speaking before we thought about what we were about to say. A person with an excellent spirit uses self-control with the words he speaks. He puts a bridle on his words and does not speak with haste.

We have experienced the one-sided conversation with someone who is devoured by the "me monster." No matter who is sharing about what, this person butts in the conversation and has a "one-up" story to share in order to get attention from other people. If you caught a big fish, he caught one bigger. If you had two cavities filled, he had six. If you share about an accident, he had three accidents in one day. He can top anything anyone shares. He thinks he has to speak to every conversation. He believes his opinion matters above others. In reality he reveals his ignorance.

It is a fruit-bearing exercise to just hold your tongue in some conversations and not have to give your opinion or experience. Be sensitive today to the times where you interrupt someone in a conversation or on the phone. Holding your tongue is a discipline you will benefit from and we all would do well to practice. Practice this discipline this today and see how it feels.

DAILY JOURNAL

1. What is the Lord speaking to me through these verses?

_____

_____

_____

2. Were there any particular words that came out of my mouth today that I need to repent of? I ask the Holy Spirit to touch my heart and keep these words out of my mouth tomorrow.

_____

_____

_____

3. Where did I use restraint today in my speech with others?

_____

_____

_____

Day 22

USE WORDS THAT FREE

You are snared with the words of your mouth; you are taken with the words of your mouth. Do this now, my son, and deliver yourself; when you have come into the hand of your friend, go and humble yourself; plead with your friend!
—PROVERBS 6:2–3

Key words: You are snared with the words of your mouth.

THE SCRIPTURAL CONTEXT of this passage is an admonition to not become one who owes money. However, the encouragement of these verses applies to many areas of our lives. We are snared with the words of our mouths. We are caught red-handed by the words that pass through our lips. We think we believe one way, but our words reveal what is really inside. We believe we are pious and holy, but our words reveal a different heart—one that is wicked.

If we are not careful and prayerful, we can be trapped by our words. They call it a trap because it catches you unaware and it is hard to get out of. It is usually a painful experience to get out of a trap. It costs something, emotionally and often financially.

As a manager of people at a Christian organization, I can't tell you the number of times I had very responsible people under my charge—people who were seasoned, well-educated, having the appearance of maturity—say the most inane, unbelievably immature, and caustic words to others. Then they would spend every ounce of their energy trying to convince me that they didn't say those things (when they probably did) or that they really didn't mean it like it sounded; surely they were misunderstood. The problem is that with some of these people, I had this very conversation on more than one occasion. Often it ended up being their word against another's word. They simply could not assume responsibility for their actions. There must be someone else to blame. I mean if we can't blame someone else, who is to blame?

Really there is just one acceptable response to being snared by your words: to humble yourself and repent. It is only through humbling ourselves and accepting responsibility for our words that healing and change can come to our hearts. Solomon said in today's passage that we are to go to the point of exhaustion and give our neighbor no rest to free ourselves from the entrapment of our words.

It comes down to this: How far will you go to free yourself and others from the words you have spoken that entrap you and hurt them? Will you humble yourself? Will you ask forgiveness? Will you assume responsibility for your words?

DAILY JOURNAL

1. What is the Lord speaking to me through
   these verses?

   _____

   _____

   _____

2. Were there any particular words that came
   out of my mouth today that I need to repent
   of? I ask the Holy Spirit to touch my heart
   and keep these words out of my mouth
   tomorrow.

   _____

   _____

   _____

3. How am I making an effort to free myself
   and others with my words?

   _____

   _____

   _____

Day 23

THE TAMING WORK

But no man can tame the tongue. It is an unruly evil, full of deadly poison. With it we bless the Lord and Father, and with it we curse men, who are made in the image of God. Out of the same mouth proceed blessing and cursing. My brothers, these things ought not to be so.
—JAMES 3:8–10

Key words: these things ought not to be so

IT IS AMAZING how our mouths can speak and proclaim the things of God and His Word, praise and celebrate Him in worshipping hymns, and then turn around to slander, blaspheme, falsely judge, criticize, complain, and even swear. How absurd that we would praise our Father and then curse His creations made in His likeness!

We have heard the many quips about the poison that can come from the tongue:

Loose tongues are worse than wicked hands.
—A JEWISH PROVERB

She had a poison tongue.
—ANONYMOUS

'Tis slander,
Whose edge is sharper than the sword, whose
tongue

> Outvenoms all the worms of Nile, whose
>   breath
> Rides on the posting winds, and doth belie
> All corners of the world. Kings, queens, and
>   states,
> Maids, matrons, nay, the secrets of the grave
> This viperous slander enters.[1]
>
> —SHAKESPEARE

A great challenge and opportunity lies before us to cry out to the Lord for the power to tame the most unruly member of our body, the tongue. Taming the tongue is simply something we cannot do by ourselves in the flesh. The day's scripture is quite clear here; no human being can tame the tongue. However, we have a hope: the power of the Holy Spirit in our lives that gives us a way for our words and our walk to be one and the same. As Paul teaches, "If we live in the Spirit, let us also walk in the Spirit" (Gal. 5:25).

Few things reveal more about our relationships with Jesus than the words that come out of our mouths. The Lord wants there to be a symmetry or congruency in all the areas of our lives—the words we speak to men in symmetry with the words we speak to Him; our secret lives congruent with our public lives; our thoughts and actions in sync with one another—and in all things bringing Him glory.

DAILY JOURNAL

1. What is the Lord speaking to me through these verses?

   _____

   _____

   _____

2. Were there any particular words that came out of my mouth today that I need to repent of? I ask the Holy Spirit to touch my heart and keep these words out of my mouth tomorrow.

   _____

   _____

   _____

3. What am I noticing about God's help in taming my tongue?

   _____

   _____

   _____

Day 24

CRY IN YOUR DISTRESS

I cried to the LORD with my voice, and He
answered me from His holy hill. Selah.
—PSALM 3:4

Key words: He answered me.

HOW DO YOU respond to adversity, severe trauma, deep affliction, or other unforeseen ills that impact you, your family, or loved ones? There are traumatic events in life that stop us completely in our tracks. Time stands still, and all at once nothing else matters. When my four-year-old and I were in an accident that almost claimed her life, left her in a coma for weeks, and in the hospital for months, my wife and I cried out to the Lord with everything that was within us. When another daughter was born three months premature and spent three months in the perinatal center clinging to life, our voices cried for help day and night. Many of you have experienced even more challenging circumstances.

What are the words that come out of your mouth during such distressing and painful events? Are they words of anger, cursing, or blame of those who caused such harrowing happenstances? Do you complain? Are you negative? Are you hopeless?

Who is the first person you turn to in these dreadful

experiences with your cries for help? Do you run to the doctor first? Do you call friends, ministers, and those closest to you? Or do you do as the psalmist did and cry out to the Lord?

If we cry out to the Lord first with our words when we are faced with these life-changing events, we are expressing a deep faith that we believe God alone can act on our behalf. We are not casting ourselves on Him after we have exhausted all other alternatives. No, we are telling our Lord first and foremost that we are looking to Him for help. He is our hope. The Lord may use many people, doctors, and others to assist us in these situations; however, we should call on Him first in our day of trouble, just as He has instructed us: "Call on Me in the day of trouble; I will deliver you, and you will glorify Me" (Ps. 50:15).

When we cry out to the Lord in brokenness and humility, we are telling the Lord that He alone is able to help us. We see that; we know that. It is this kind of humility that catches the Lord's ear. The psalmist says, "You, LORD, hear the desire of the afflicted; you encourage them, and you listen to their cry" (Ps. 10:17, NIV).

The beauty of crying out to the Lord is that He answers! As we submit our words to Him during this forty-day word fast, we are submitting every word that comes out of our mouths on every occasion—in times of anger, times of sadness, times of disbelief, times of confusion, and times of great distress. Our cries can be holy cries that tell Him and Him alone, "You are my God. In You alone I am trusting."

We have some great examples in the scriptures of those who cried out to the Lord, and the encouragement also that the Lord answered their cries.

- Bartimaeus, who was blind, cried out to the Lord for mercy and was healed (Mark 10:46–52).
- The disciples of Jesus cried out to Him when they thought they were going to drown in a storm, and He saved them (Luke 8:23–24).
- Isaiah and King Hezekiah cried out to heaven and were delivered from the king of Assyria (2 Chron. 32:20–21).
- Elijah cried unto the Lord and the life of a child was restored (1 Kings 17:20–22).

Let's join these who trusted the Lord in such dire circumstances and always cry out to the Lord first.

DAILY JOURNAL

1. What is the Lord speaking to me through these verses?

_____

_____

_____

2. Were there any particular words that came out of my mouth today that I need to repent of? I ask the Holy Spirit to touch my heart and keep these words out of my mouth tomorrow.

_____

_____

_____

3. How is grumbling and complaining different from crying out to the Lord?

_____

_____

_____

DO YOUR WORDS BUILD?

The Spirit of the LORD spoke by me, and
His word was on my tongue.
—2 SAMUEL 23:2

Key words: His word was on my
tongue

HAVE YOU EVER had the experience of speaking something categorically inspiring? There are few things that compare to delivering a life-giving word of encouragement to someone else, and you know that by the clarity, the excellence, and the beauty of the words, they were not your own but from the Holy Spirit.

First Corinthians 14:1 says, "Follow the way of love and eagerly desire gifts of the Spirit, especially prophecy" (NIV). Verse 3 goes on to instruct, "But the one who prophesies speaks to people for their strengthening, encouraging and comfort" (NIV). I acknowledge there is much controversy about spiritual gifts, in particular prophecy. But I believe prophecy as it is used in this context isn't telling of things to come in the future but simply edifies others. It is the Spirit of God speaking through us to give His words of life and the Spirit to others. *Strengthening* is an architectural term used in this passage to mean "building others up in the church to support them."[1] *Encouraging* means to motivate and cause others to pursue the Lord with greater zeal, to spur others on to greater depths in their relationship with Christ. *Comfort* in the context of this verse simply means to console others during trials, to speak words of life to those who are suffering.

As believers we have the Holy Spirit in us. If we make it our heart's desire to speak words of strengthening, encouragement, and consolation, then we can have the Lord speak through us. Can you imagine the wonderful, life-giving words He wants to speak to others through us?

What words, then, should be on our tongue instead of negative, damaging words? Ah, words of support, encouragement, and comfort to many. Oh, how glorious to speak these words to others rather than judgments, criticism, sarcasm, negativity, complaint, or gossip! Others may speak these words, but let them not come from us.

DAILY JOURNAL

1. What is the Lord speaking to me through these verses?

   _____

   _____

   _____

2. Were there any particular words that came out of my mouth today that I need to repent of? I ask the Holy Spirit to touch my heart

and keep these words out of my mouth
tomorrow.

_____

_____

_____

3. Where did I speak a word of encouragement
   to someone today?

_____

_____

_____

Day 26

NO MATTER HOW SMALL

My lips certainly will not speak unjustly, nor will my tongue mutter deceit.
—JOB 27:4, NAS

Key words: nor will my tongue mutter deceit

I LOVE SO MANY things about my wife. One of her more admirable character traits is that she is exacting. She likes things done thoroughly. She likes things done accurately. I have to confess that her example is just what I have needed to understand that the Lord requires accuracy in the words that come from my mouth. He wants our words to be precise and truthful, with no deceit and no exaggeration.

The issue I personally struggled with in the past was distorting the truth by exaggerating. It's not that I wasn't telling the truth; I was just stretching the truth to make stories, situations, or experiences more exciting. A more socially acceptable term is *embellishing*. But in the end it's still a type of deceit.

We live in a world that distorts the truth and deals in degrees of truth. In the political realm it is so difficult to distinguish between the truth and what is false. Rival political parties blame each other for twisting the truth, distorting the truth, being two-faced, and on and on. It seems that the more highly skilled you are at dodging the truth and stretching the truth, the brighter your future in politics.

However, this does not just happens in politics. We live with degrees of truth in all facets of our world today. There is a whole plagiarism technology industry that has emerged to address academic integrity. Rarely does a week go by that we don't read about a famous reporter or writer being exposed for plagiarism or a musician suing for copyright infringement.

Furthermore, all of us are too familiar with the following idioms:

- A little white lie
- Fudging
- Fibbing
- Twisting the truth
- Stretching the truth

Regardless of how great or how small, it is all the same; it is distorting the truth. And it is not what the Lord wants coming out of our mouths. The psalms say, "You desire truth in the inward parts, and in the hidden part You make me to know wisdom" (Ps. 51:6). Call it fact, integrity, honesty, or whatever you want, the Lord desires us to walk in truth outwardly with others and inwardly in our hearts. The Lord takes great delight in the truth, as Proverbs teaches: "Lying lips are abomination to the LORD, but those who deal truly are His delight" (Prov. 12:22).

Take a serious inventory today about the precision and truthfulness of the words that move across your lips.

DAILY JOURNAL

1. What is the Lord speaking to me through these verses?

_____

_____

_____

2. Were there any particular words that came out of my mouth today that I need to repent of? I ask the Holy Spirit to touch my heart and keep these words out of my mouth tomorrow.

_____

_____

_____

3. Where do I exaggerate?

_____

_____

_____

Day 27

KEEP YOUR WORD

But above all things, my brothers, do not swear,
either by heaven or by the earth or by any other
oath. But let your "Yes" be "Yes" and your "No"
be "No," that you do not fall into condemnation.
—JAMES 5:12

Key words: But let your "Yes" be
"Yes" and your "No" be "No."

WE LIVE IN a culture where contracts have little meaning. We see a similar event almost every day in the news: "College coach signs three-year extension on contract." Then a week later they break the contract and sign with another school for more money.

Not only have contracts lost their importance in the world, but also Christians seem to be no exception. I spent my last fifteen work years in a profession where people regularly broke contracts. They gave me their word to do something, signed a contract, then at the last moment found something better and broke the contract. All of them were Christians.

Many of us have had a similar firsthand experience. Maybe a Christian brother in business gives his word to another Christian brother, then backs out of his word at serious cost and suffering to the other brother. When confronted, he gives this response: "It's different.

This is business." There seems to be a perverted rule of engagement—a double standard—among Christians in business that somehow the Christian principles of the Scriptures don't apply to business.

However, the Word of the Lord is clear for believers and unbelievers alike. Our word means something. When we say we're going to do something, we need to live up to our word. When we say yes, it has meaning and significance. People can count on us when we give our word. It may cause us momentous pain and sacrifice to keep our word at times, but we should do everything possible to honor it. What a poor testimony it offers the world and other Christians when we give our word to do something and then back out when it gets tough.

We have to ask ourselves the question, Am I true to my word?

How recently have you committed yourself to something and then didn't finish it because it was more difficult than you anticipated? What kind of problems did it create for others when you backed out of that commitment? Most of us have had this experience of letting someone down by not keeping our word. It is a very unpleasant situation for all involved.

So, what are we supposed to do when we have given our word to do something and find out we bit off more than we could chew and are incapable of fulfilling the commitment due to other circumstances? First, we should evaluate the situation again and do everything possible to keep our word as intended. The integrity of our word is at stake. The personal hardship and pain it causes may be difficult, but it is worth making our word good.

If we see no way to keep our word, then we must go to those to whom we made the commitment and communicate our desire to fulfill our word and explore how to make that happen still. If there is absolutely no way to keep our word, then we must be humble and apologetic, and we ought to make sure we pay out of our pocket for the added expenses incurred to others by our not fulfilling the commitment made.

Most importantly ask the Lord what He wants you to learn from the experience. When the situation is most difficult, the Lord has mighty lessons to teach us, and He uses them to develop character in our lives. The Lord gives us grace and mercy, but the Lord does not give us character. That's something that builds through the choices we make.

DAILY JOURNAL

1. What is the Lord speaking to me through these verses?

   _____

   _____

   _____

2. Were there any particular words that came out of my mouth today that I need to repent of? I ask the Holy Spirit to touch my heart

and keep these words out of my mouth tomorrow.

_____

_____

_____

3. When have I gone back on my word? How can I make amends for it?

_____

_____

_____

Day 28

In What Do You Boast?

Some boast in chariots and some in horses, but we
will boast in the name of the LORD, our God.
—Psalm 20:7, nas

Key words: but we will boast in the
name of the LORD, our God

THE PSALMIST HERE observed that people of the
world at that time boasted in chariots and speedy horses.
Today we might boast in luxurious and fast sports cars.
Times change, but the pride of life doesn't. People who
are of the world boast in the pride of possessions. There
is an abundance of "stuff" to boast in: fortunes, great
mansions, momentous stock holdings, luxury homes,
superior intellect and education, or military might.

What do you boast in? Should you even boast at all?
I love the Word and its practical application to our daily
lives. Even in matters such as this the Scriptures are rel-
evant and instructive. The answer? Don't toot your own
horn: "Do not lift up your horn on high, do not speak
with insolent pride" (Ps. 75:5, nas). If praise comes to us,
where should it come from? From others, not ourselves:
"Let another man praise you, and not your own mouth;
a stranger, and not your own lips" (Prov. 27:2).

We should boast in the Lord, our strength and
salvation. And we have plenty to boast about when

it comes to our Lord! He has done for us what we cannot do. As Isaiah says, "I will greatly rejoice in the LORD, my soul shall be joyful in my God; for He has clothed me with the garments of salvation, He has covered me with the robe of righteousness, as a bridegroom decks himself with ornaments, and as a bride adorns herself with her jewels" (Isa. 61:10).

The context of our passage for today from Psalm 20:7 is fully understood by looking at verse 6: "Now this I know: The LORD gives victory to his anointed. He answers him from his heavenly sanctuary with the victorious power of his right hand" (NIV). This is what the psalmist was saying in verse 7—we boast in the Lord because He answers our prayers. When we cry out to the Lord, He hears us from His holy heaven and answers with the saving strength of His right hand. Hallelujah! There is truly none other like our Lord: "O LORD God of Israel, there is no God like You in the heavens or on the earth, who keeps covenants and mercy with Your servants who walk before You with all their heart" (2 Chron. 6:14, NIV).

DAILY JOURNAL

1. What is the Lord speaking to me through these verses?

_____

_____

_____

2. Were there any particular words that came out of my mouth today that I need to repent of? I ask the Holy Spirit to touch my heart and keep these words out of my mouth tomorrow.

_____

_____

_____

3. Does my reputation reflect a boastful person? If so, how can I become more humble?

_____

_____

_____

Day 29

What Do Your Lips Preserve?

That you may regard discretion, and that
your lips may keep knowledge.
—Proverbs 5:2

Key words: your lips may keep
knowledge

OH, THAT OUR lips would keep knowledge and speak the words the Lord desires spoken! From our lips can come words that preserve others and us or bring great harm to many people.

In the Old Testament the priest's lips would preserve knowledge, and men had to seek instruction from him only. The priest was the messenger of God himself: "For a priest's lips should preserve knowledge, and people should seek the law from his mouth; for he is the messenger of the LORD of Hosts" (Mal. 2:7, NIV). But praise God—in Christ we are all made priests to our God. In Him, we have access to the mind and words of Christ: "...and from Jesus Christ, who is the faithful witness, the firstborn from the dead, and the ruler of the kings of the earth. To Him who loved us and washed us from our sins in His own blood, and has made us kings and priests to His God and Father, to Him be glory and dominion forever and ever. Amen" (Rev. 1:5–6).

So as we have knowledge preserved within us, the Lord wants us to tell others of His marvelous saving power and grace. Can we control the words that come across our lips? Yes, by the power of the Holy Spirit we can constrain our tongue and then speak His words. It is because of the price Christ paid on the cross that the Holy Spirit is available to us. Christ left that we might do greater works (John 14:12), and one of these greater works is that we are empowered to speak His words, not ours, and constrain this wildfire, the tongue.

The passage today also speaks of discretion. This is one of my favorite words. It embodies so many different facets of wisdom: prudence, sensitivity, knowing when to keep silent, and understanding when to not get involved. Discretion is akin to someone who is skilled in driving. They know when to go; they know when to apply the brakes ever so gently at one time and coming to a full stop at another. Discretion is wisdom in action, allowing you to live your life and guard the words that cross your lips. Discretion saves us from sin. A lack of discretion will get a person into great trouble.

DAILY JOURNAL

1. What is the Lord speaking to me through these verses?

   _____

   _____

   _____

2. Were there any particular words that came out of my mouth today that I need to repent of? I ask the Holy Spirit to touch my heart and keep these words out of my mouth tomorrow.

   _____

   _____

   _____

3. How did I demonstrate discretion with my speech today?

   _____

   _____

   _____

Day 30

WOULD YOU PASS THE EXAM?

Though you probe my heart, though you examine me at night and test me, you will find that I have planned no evil; my mouth has not transgressed.
—PSALM 17:3, NIV

Key words: my mouth has not transgressed

THE PSALMIST CHRONICLES how the Lord visited him and inspected his character, or examined him. The word *examine* here reminds me of the examination room where a doctor gives a thorough checkup. This verse denotes the Lord coming for the purpose of inspection. In the night, in solitude and darkness, when the psalmist was alone, in a time when what we really are can be seen, there the Lord examined and tested him and found nothing evil. An amazing thought! I've heard this saying repeatedly: "Your reputation is what others think you are; your character is what you really are." The psalmist's character was pristine.

Then the psalmist takes it even further. As much as he may have been provoked and injured by others, he was determined not to retaliate or to give anything but a response that would meet God's approval. He purposed that only words that are acceptable to God would come from his lips. What a wonderful thought, to know that God has so empowered us through the Holy Spirit that we can be silent and not strike back at others with our words, that when we speak, our words will be pleasing to the God of the universe.

It is good for the Lord to test us. His testing purifies us and removes all the dross of sin and selfishness, and His testing cleanses our words. Difficult circumstances come our way for many reasons: we make mistakes and receive the consequences; others purpose to hurt us; the enemy is out to steal, kill, and destroy us; and the Lord is testing us. Again, the Lord tests us to purify us. He also tests us to see if we are trustworthy. He wants to promote us to more responsibility in spiritual matters and needs to know we are faithful and trustworthy to handle it. Let us be as the psalmist and invite the testing of the Lord. Let us pray as David prayed: "Search me, God, and know my heart; test me and know my anxious thoughts. See if there is any offensive way in me, and lead me in the way everlasting" (Ps. 139:23–24, NIV).

Let us purpose today that by the power of the Holy Spirit, we will not transgress with our mouths.

DAILY JOURNAL

1. What is the Lord speaking to me through these verses?

   _____

   _____

   _____

2. Were there any particular words that came out of my mouth today that I need to repent of? I ask the Holy Spirit to touch my heart and keep these words out of my mouth tomorrow.

   _____

   _____

   _____

3. Does my character match my reputation?

   _____

   _____

   _____

THE HEART OF THE MATTER

The hearts of the wise make their mouths prudent, and their lips promote instruction.
—PROVERBS 16:23, NIV

Key words: the hearts of the wise

HAVE YOU EVER made a fool of yourself? How did it happen? More than likely it occurred when you opened your mouth and said the wrong thing or said something at the wrong time or in the wrong place. When it comes to saying just about anything, timing is everything. Say the right thing at the wrong time and the effect will often be a big *thud*.

However, the heart of a wise person teaches his mouth what to say, when to say it, and before whom to speak. The wise person's heart will be full of all the words that need to be spoken. He will not be at a loss for what to say or how to say it. This is the fruit of wisdom.

Prudence in speech doesn't mean eloquence in speech. It is not the eloquence of words that determines the impact of a discourse, nor is it the quantity of words that communicates the greatest effect of thought. Rather, it is the heart of wisdom that creates the impetus for rich, meaningful conversation. Again, the Sermon on the Mount carries approximately 2,000 words. It's a very short discourse. Lincoln's Gettysburg Address has even fewer—just 272 words. Enough said.

There is one sure way to not be made a fool of: be silent. However, there are times we are expected to speak and the Lord wants us to speak with wisdom. In those times our speech reveals what is in our hearts. What is in our hearts can be emptiness, foolishness, wisdom of the world, or wisdom from above.

The way to wisdom is through God alone. Godly wisdom is not gained from education, worldly experience, or heredity. It's gained this way: "The fear of the Lord is the beginning of wisdom, and the knowledge of the Holy One is understanding" (Prov. 9:10, NIV). The heart of a wise person considers what comes out of his mouth. He doesn't blurt things out. When he has a word of wisdom, he even considers to whom he gives it: "Do not give what is holy to the dogs, nor throw your pearls before swine, lest they trample them under their feet and turn around and attack you" (Matt. 7:6). The word *dogs* here is a very graphic representation of those who don't respond in a positive way to the words of truth. When the heart of wisdom richly dwells within you, it directs you and keeps you from speaking foolishly, and it also instructs you whom to persuade or teach.

DAILY JOURNAL

1. What is the Lord speaking to me through these verses?

   _____

   _____

   _____

2. Were there any particular words that came out of my mouth today that I need to repent of? I ask the Holy Spirit to touch my heart and keep these words out of my mouth tomorrow.

   _____

   _____

   _____

3. How is wisdom showing in my speech?

   _____

   _____

   _____

Day 32

WHAT'S TASTY TO YOU?

*Gracious words are a honeycomb, sweet to
the soul and healing to the bones.*
—PROVERBS 16:24, NIV

Key words: sweet to the soul

IF YOU HAVE developed a taste for the Word of the
Lord, then you know how sweet it can be. The Scriptures reveal how tasty the Word of the Lord is and
allude to us literally devouring it. But we can be very
finicky and discriminatory in our taste for food. And
there are so many foods to choose from! I believe
the Scriptures are like everything else in life that we
consume; we have to develop a taste for it. When we
develop a taste for the Word, it can become more
desirable, fulfilling, and delightful to our souls than
food to our bodies.

The Scriptures speak of it this way:

> How sweet are Your words to the taste of my
> mouth! Sweeter than honey to my mouth!
>
> —PSALM 119:103

> Oh, taste and see that the LORD is good;
> blessed is the man who takes refuge in Him.
>
> —PSALM 34:8

I have not departed from the commandment
of His lips; I have esteemed the words of His
mouth more than my necessary food.

—Job 23:12

Your words were found and I ate them. And
Your word became to me the joy and rejoicing
of my heart, for I am called by Your name, O
Lord God of Hosts.

—Jeremiah 15:16

These scriptures prompt this question: Have you developed a taste for the Word of God?

And what about your own words? Pleasant words are sweet to us and also to those around us. They are like the honey of the honeycomb too. Words of acceptance, affirmation, encouragement, positivity, gratefulness, and praise are sweet to the souls of people and bring healing. Are you speaking these words to others?

Pleasant words that we receive or speak are sweet to the mind, emotions, and will. Also, they are healing to our bones, those parts of our anatomy that hold up everything else in our bodies. Contrast negative words with these pleasant words. Negative words are bitter and unpleasant to our souls.

Most of us are aware of the medical term *the placebo effect*. It's the phenomenon where a person takes a fake substance and his medical condition improves because the person expects the treatment to help. Psychologists have been telling us about it for many years in clinical trials. It is real. There have been scores of studies on the validity of the placebo effect.

Psychologists now also talk about *the nocebo effect*. Words and expectations can impact our bodies to heal or harm us. And in recent years doctors have started to do research that recognizes the validity of this nocebo effect. The nocebo effect for doctors means that they acknowledge there is power in the words they speak, power to encourage healing or power to unintentionally impede the healing process.[1]

Think about it. You are with a nurse, and she says, "You are a high-risk patient." Medical science is now saying these kinds of statements can negatively impact the physical health of patients. I love it when secular, professional people come to conclusions that Scripture already teaches us! In this instance it is another confirmation that we need to remove the words of judgment, criticism, sarcasm, negativity, complaining, and gossip from our language.

Christians are carriers. We should be carriers of healing and encouraging words. The Lord wants you to go and infect others today with these words of life!

DAILY JOURNAL

1. What is the Lord speaking to me through these verses?

   _____

   _____

   _____

2. Were there any particular words that came out of my mouth today that I need to repent of? I ask the Holy Spirit to touch my heart and keep these words out of my mouth tomorrow.

_____

_____

_____

3. How are my words offering sweetness like honey to others?

_____

_____

_____

WORTHLESS RELIGION

Those who consider themselves religious and yet do not keep a tight rein on their tongues deceive themselves, and their religion is worthless.
—JAMES 1:26, NIV

Key words: their religion is worthless

MANY ASPECTS OF a person's persona may suggest the existence of religion in their heart, yet one thing reveals all other appearances as worthless. If a person does not restrain the propensity to sin with their tongue, then they don't have authentic faith.

Think about it. According to the writings of James, under the unction of the Holy Spirit, whatever love, zeal for prayer, or personal spiritual gifting a person may have, this one sinful propensity—not bridling one's tongue—neutralizes it all. That man or woman's religion is in vain.

It's amazing to think of the amount of effort, time, and perhaps money that may go into creating the illusion of piety in such a life, all for naught. It's all worthless if one cannot bridle the tongue. When we hear people judging others, being critical or sarcastic, speaking negative words, complaining, or gossiping, we know their religion is worthless. Furthermore, with worthless religion, there's a lot of performing in order to appear righteous in the eyes of other people. This is the "deceiving themselves" part of it. When a person walks in deception, he or she tries, in great futility, to appear religious.

Deception is a difficult condition to address in a life. Our enemy, the devil, doesn't need to concern himself with a person who is deceived. They have led themselves down a path that does not lead to the kingdom of God.

All of these thoughts should compel us to shout out to the Holy Spirit to empower us to bring our words to the foot of the cross. Let us cry out, in the spirit of Isaiah, "Lord Jesus, send that seraphim down from the throne of God and let it exact its work quickly and thoroughly upon my mouth. I need your help!" (See Isaiah 6:6–7.)

DAILY JOURNAL

1. What is the Lord speaking to me through these verses?

   _____

   _____

   _____

2. Were there any particular words that came out of my mouth today that I need to repent of? I ask the Holy Spirit to touch my heart

and keep these words out of my mouth tomorrow.

_____

_____

_____

3. In what way, if any, is the deception of worthless religion at work in my life?

_____

_____

_____

LISTEN WELL

Therefore, my beloved brothers, let every man be
swift to hear, slow to speak, and slow to anger.
—JAMES 1:19

Key words: swift to hear, slow to
speak

MOST OF US know someone who is a great listener. That person has a unique ability to focus on you as if you were vitally important to them. They put you at ease and draw conversation out of you from a level deep in your soul.

I can tell you about an experience I've had with this kind of person. Some years ago I was invited to a luncheon where John Maxwell was speaking. A friend of mine invited me to sit at the head table with John and five others. I arrived early to the luncheon, and John was already sitting at our table, so I had the occasion to visit with him for about fifteen minutes one on one. Later in the day when I reflected on my time with him, I realized he had turned our entire conversation into an opportunity for him to learn whatever I could tell him about my area of expertise, which is Christian education. He asked a few pointed questions, inquired now and then as I spoke, and listened intently. He drew thoughts out of me that I don't normally share with people. I have never been around someone who was so skilled at the art of listening!

Being a good listener isn't as simple as it seems. You have to ask thoughtful questions, empathize with the other person, and, most importantly, be slow to speak. There is great safety and wisdom in being slow to speak. When in doubt, don't speak. And when you think you have something to say, commit it to the Lord and ask His Holy Spirit to sift your thoughts and words and take it slow. Being slow to speak frees you to be able to listen. When you give a person your full attention, you send them a clear message: *I value your words.*

We teach so much in education about the different ways to communicate: writing, reading, speaking (which includes nonverbal communication), visual communication (plays, visual technology, etc.). However, I have long bemoaned that we don't teach how to be good listeners, one of the most important skills in communicating and building relationships.

It doesn't take a dissertation of spoken words to address an issue or explain a point. It takes a word spoken in due season, a word spoken just at the right time. Even a single word can unlock mysteries, flood a person with encouragement, or bring the light of God to an issue. There is often a precursor to being able to give a person a word that encourages and helps them along in their life, and that precursor is just listening—really hearing them.

DAILY JOURNAL

1. What is the Lord speaking to me through these verses?

   _____

   _____

   _____

2. Were there any particular words that came out of my mouth today that I need to repent of? I ask the Holy Spirit to touch my heart and keep these words out of my mouth tomorrow.

   _____

   _____

   _____

3. Where did I take the time to really listen to someone today and give him or her my full attention?

   _____

   _____

   _____

CAN YOU KEEP A SECRET?

A gossip betrays a confidence, but a trust-worthy person keeps a secret.
—**PROVERBS 11:13, NIV**

Key words: keeps a secret

WHAT SHOULD BE your response when someone comes to you with a secret? You want to be approachable and safe for others to share information with you, but you don't want to give a listening ear to gossip. If someone comes to you and wants to share a secret about another person with you, then it might be gossip. Therefore an appropriate response could be something similar to this: "If it has anything to do with information about another person that is personal, then I really shouldn't hear it." If a friend wants to share a personal secret with you, then listen if you can pray for them and give encouragement.

I truly believe just being honest and straightforward with people in a gentle manner would put a stop to most gossip before it begins. However, if you decide to hear a friend's prayer request or confession of sin, you have to ask yourself the following question: "Can I keep a confidence, 100 percent?"

Our fellowship with other people is based on confidence. That fellowship is precious, and one of the most important decisions we can make to ensure the integrity of our relationships is to practice confidentiality. The scripture is explicit about this in today's passage. If we hear personal information in order to pray about it or pray for someone confessing sin to us, we cannot share it with anyone else. That means not sharing it with someone else for them to pray with us, not sharing it with a prayer group, not sharing it with anyone.

This is one of the greatest tests of life: Can we be counted on to be a person who knows how to keep a confidence? The person who can keep a confidence will be sought out for friendship and counsel. I often use my wife as an example. Annamae is a woman who knows how to keep a confidence, plus she is a bearer of truth, mercy, and grace. Because of these character qualities in her, women seek her out for friendship, and she is a marvelous friend. She can be trusted to keep a matter with 100 percent confidentiality. A trustworthy person can do this.

DAILY JOURNAL

1. What is the Lord speaking to me through these verses?

_____

_____

_____

2. Were there any particular words that came out of my mouth today that I need to repent

of? I ask the Holy Spirit to touch my heart
and keep these words out of my mouth
tomorrow.

_____

_____

_____

3. How have I shown myself to be a person
who can or can't keep a confidence?

_____

_____

_____

Day 36

DO YOUR WORDS NOURISH?

*The lips of the righteous feed many, but
fools die for lack of wisdom.*
—PROVERBS 10:21

Key words: the lips of the righteous
feed many

THE LIPS OF a righteous person give encouragement, counsel, and consolation to those who are hungry in spirit. There are no treasures on earth that compare with the wisdom and understanding that comes from the Spirit when our tongues are submitted to Him. Spiritual wisdom establishes a person as a blessing for many souls.

A righteous man's words will be like a perpetual fountain of life to everyone he comes across. The righteous person's words will feed a needy soul just like food feeds our bodies, just like cold water quenches our thirst. The words of the righteous give the "bread of life" to the hungry of spirit. As the loaves and fishes multiplied to feed the five thousand, so the lips of the righteous person give spiritual words of nourishment to as many who will hear his words and believe. The Lord Himself promised, "Blessed are those who hunger and thirst for righteousness, for they shall be filled" (Matt. 5:6).

The fool, for a lack of common sense, dies a spiritual death. Words of life that feed the spirit are put before him, but his heart is drawn away from spiritual nourishment by his worldly desires. The fool dries up spiritually and is destroyed. This is a matter of life and death: "See, today I have set before you life and prosperity, and death and disaster. What I am commanding you today is to love the LORD your God, to walk in His ways, and to keep His commandments and His statutes and His judgments, so that you may live and multiply. Then the LORD your God will bless you in the land which you go to possess." (Deut. 30:15–16).

From God alone comes true spiritual food and springs of living water. However, we have to choose to open our spirits and partake of a full supply. He sends His words to us through the words of those who have learned to listen to Him. Our pursuit of the Lord is really so simple, even a child can understand it. If you are hungry, come to the table and eat. Seek the Lord, and you will find Him.

DAILY JOURNAL

1. What is the Lord speaking to me through these verses?

_____

_____

_____

2. Were there any particular words that came out of my mouth today that I need to repent of? I ask the Holy Spirit to touch my heart and keep these words out of my mouth tomorrow.

_____

_____

_____

3. How would I describe the kind of nourishment my words offer others?

_____

_____

_____

WHAT DO YOU HEAR
WHEN YOU LISTEN?

For I have not spoken on My own authority, but the Father
who sent Me gave Me a command, what I should say and
what I should speak. I know that His command is eternal
life. Therefore what I say, I say as the Father tells me.
—JOHN 12:49–50

Key words: gave Me a command,
what I should say

IT IS NOT too mystical or implausible to think that
we could speak the words of the Lord. It should be
fearful and completely humbling to say to someone,
"I believe this is what the Lord wants you to hear in
this situation." Jesus said, "Whatever I say is just what
the Father has told me to say" (John 12:50, NIV). How
did Jesus come to the place where He could speak the
Father's words? I believe it was through His intimate
relationship with the Father. He heard the Father's
words.

How do you get to know someone? You spend time
with them and have a dialogue. However, you should
spend more time listening than talking. You don't get to
know someone by talking to him or her about yourself.

What makes us poor listeners? I believe our listening skills are thwarted by a far too high opinion of

ourselves, otherwise known as pride. We think others need to hear the words we have to say, but in reality the most important gift we can offer a Christian brother or sister is simply the service of listening. Someone who can't make time to listen to a fellow Christian will eventually not be able to make time to listen to the Lord.

With the curtailment of so many negative and frivolous words being spoken from my mouth, I have started listening a great deal more to people. More importantly I have discovered that prayer is most alive and intimate when listening as opposed to talking. We are in a better position to hear Jesus and know Him by being quiet and listening in prayer. It's just as the psalm says: "Be still and know that I am God; I will be exalted among the nations, I will be exalted in the earth" (Ps. 46:10).

Have you ever read the opinion section of a local newspaper? It's where people get an opportunity to share their opinions on a topic. Some of the thoughts people share in print are embarrassing, horribly hurtful, and judgmental, and they very often reveal their significant lack of factual information, or ignorance, of a topic. We have all heard the phrases:

- "This is my two cents' worth."
- "Everybody has an opinion."
- "They pooled their ignorance on the topic."

If we want to be able to speak the words of God, the first requirement is to begin to listen and hear His words. Our personal opinions and thoughts are limited in their ability to bring life and freedom to people. The most important place that listening happens is in prayer.

DAILY JOURNAL

1. What is the Lord speaking to me through these verses?

   _____

   _____

   _____

2. Were there any particular words that came out of my mouth today that I need to repent of? I ask the Holy Spirit to touch my heart and keep these words out of my mouth tomorrow.

   _____

   _____

   _____

3. What keeps me from sitting quietly before the Lord in prayer?

   _____

   _____

   _____

DO YOU SHARE THE GOSPEL?

*My mouth will declare Your righteousness and Your sal-
vation all the day, for I cannot know their numbers.*
—PSALM 71:15

Key words: My mouth will declare
Your righteousness and Your salvation

IS IT REALLY my job to tell others about Jesus? Isn't
that what the evangelist is for? I just don't have that gift.

Most of us have had these and so many more thoughts
in response to the invitation to proclaim the benefits of
following Jesus to others. What keeps us from sharing
our faith with others? Pride. We're worried about our
reputation. We're too influenced by the world. We're
afraid of being politically incorrect. Maybe others will
think we're fanatics. Maybe we don't share with others
because we feel as if we're hypocrites.

There are myriad reasons we could find to not share
the gospel with others. However, I believe these are
just excuses for most of us.

The truth is we're obligated to share the love of Jesus
with nonbelievers. There are repeated, clear directives
given in the Scriptures, such as, "But you are a chosen
race, a royal priesthood, a holy nation, a people for
God's own possession, so that you may declare the
goodness of Him who has called you out of darkness into His marvelous light" (1 Pet. 2:9). However,

if your motivation for doing something is because you are obligated, then your corresponding level of passion is usually fairly low for that task. Rather, we should count it a privilege to be able to deliver the good news to those who don't know Christ as their Savior.

Jesus came to bring the good news to those who were sick and dying physically and spiritually. He poured His life into His disciples, but it was those who didn't know the good news that He came to seek and save, and He was no respecter of people: "While Jesus sat at supper in the house, many tax collectors and sinners came and sat down with Him and His disciples. When the Pharisees saw it, they said to His disciples, 'Why does your Teacher eat with tax collectors and sinners?' But when Jesus heard that, He said to them, 'Those who are well do not need a physician, but those who are sick'" (Matt. 9:10–12).

I believe we have a misconception that sharing the gospel is going to be offensive to others and equally embarrassing to us. I am convinced that as we allow the Lord to change our hearts and words, the Spirit of God will bring forth a new word from our lips. And as we speak the words that the Spirit of God would have us speak, they will be pleasant, full of grace, and life giving. There is no guarantee our words will be received, but we will always be planting the seeds of the gospel when the words that come from our mouths tell of His great salvation. It is with tenderness and respect that the Lord would have us give witness to His magnificent deeds all the day long with those we come into contact: "But in your hearts revere Christ as Lord. Always be prepared to give an answer to everyone who asks you to give the reason for the hope that you have. But do this with gentleness and respect" (1 Pet. 3:15).

DAILY JOURNAL

1. What is the Lord speaking to me through these verses?

_____

_____

_____

2. Were there any particular words that came out of my mouth today that I need to repent of? I ask the Holy Spirit to touch my heart and keep these words out of my mouth tomorrow.

_____

_____

_____

3. Can you remember the last time you shared the gospel with someone? What was it like for you?

_____

_____

_____

Day 39

THE FRUIT OF KINDNESS

*She opens her mouth with wisdom, and in
her tongue is the teaching of kindness.*
—PROVERBS 31:26

Key words: in her tongue is the
teaching of kindness

FROM THE LIPS of a godly wife and mother come so many different life-giving words: pronouncements of truth, words of encouragement, and instruction, just to name a few. What is the most distinguishing characteristic of this woman? Her tongue speaks words of kindness. Though she is a manager of the house, shares life with her husband, trains her children, has intimate friends, often works outside the home, and relates to church friends and neighbors, in all of this she is gracious. She manages her house with kind words. She has words of understanding and empathy for her husband. She trains her children with words of encouragement and comfort. Her close friends and coworkers are the recipients of her ability to keep a confidence. She blesses her brother and sisters in Christ and her neighbors with godly wisdom and counsel.

This godly woman in Proverbs 31 has a meek and quiet spirit.

Now let me speak from experience about this. I've

been married forty-plus years. My sin and selfishness put my wife through some harrowing circumstances and trials. Add on five children and more than our share of trauma and challenges, and my wife has had sufficient opportunities to develop a negative, pessimistic outlook on life. But that is not my wife. She is positive, godly, and sought out by others for counsel. Our children and I rise up and call her blessed.

The word the Lord has put on my wife's lips through these challenges is that there is a higher call for women today. There is a higher call to forgiveness, love, and endurance in the lives of all women than perhaps any time in the history of our nation. The enemy is pressing in for the destruction of Christian marriage in the United States. The most volatile spiritual battles in the family are taking place through men's repeated failures with pornography and fidelity. The call for women today is to stand resolute with words of forgiveness, love, and kindness.

However, the call isn't just for wives; the call is also for husbands, single men, single women, and youths. We live in an age when people have rejected the gospel because they haven't seen unity and authentic faith in many churches and among Christians. There is no more sincere testimony to the life of Christ than kind and compassionate followers of Jesus who live and speak words of forgiveness toward others and are led by the Holy Spirit: "We prove ourselves by our purity, our understanding, our patience, our kindness, by the Holy Spirit within us, and by our sincere love" (2 Cor. 6:6, NLT).

DAILY JOURNAL

1. What is the Lord speaking to me through
   these verses?

   _____

   _____

   _____

2. Were there any particular words that came
   out of my mouth today that I need to repent
   of? I ask the Holy Spirit to touch my heart
   and keep these words out of my mouth
   tomorrow.

   _____

   _____

   _____

3. Who do I know who lives out this teaching
   of speaking words of forgiveness, love, and
   kindness?

   _____

   _____

   _____

Day 40

BE A PERSON OF RESTORATION

*Surely you have instructed many, and you have strength-
ened the weak hands. Your words have raised up him
who was falling, and you have fortified the feeble knees.*
—JOB 4:3–4

Key words: Your words have raised
up him who was falling.

GOD'S CONSTANT STATE is a state of restoration. It's
what the Lord is best at: forgiving sin, reviving hope,
and supporting those who have stumbled.

How do you rate on the restoration scale—high or
low? Are you quick to assist a brother or sister who
has had a spiritual setback due to sin? If someone has
a financial failure due to poor management of credit
cards, it's not uncommon for Christians to volun-
teer to help restore the person. But how quickly do
Christians come to the side of a man or woman who
is having addiction issues with pornography?

It's puzzling how Christians classify sin in catego-
ries of severity. You seldom see Christians rushing to
the side of an adult who has had a failure with a sexual
sin. It is even more interesting to see what the scripture has to say about the issue of restoring those who
have had failures in sin: "Brothers, if a man is caught
in any transgression, you who are spiritual should

restore such a one in the spirit of meekness, watching yourselves, lest you also be tempted" (Gal. 6:1). Even if they are caught in *any* trespass? That's a pretty tall order for us, isn't it?

Reflect on the words likely to come out of your mouth in these situations:

- A youth leader is caught making a pass at a girl in the youth group. He is repentant and seeks forgiveness and restoration.
- A wife discovers X-rated magazines in the garage that belong to her husband.
- A man or woman, while driving under the influence of alcohol, gets in an accident that kills a person.
- A friend's daughter moves in with her boyfriend.
- Your brother's son in high school comes out as gay.

Are your words full of gentleness and restoration in these instances? Clearly, those are the kind of words the Lord wants us to speak. And He wants such humility to be operating in our lives that we recognize that without the grace of God, any of these situations listed above could be us.

Job's words supported those who stumbled, and his words gave strength to those who were easily tempted. What a wonderful testimony to the impact of his words. One of the lessons to learn here is that there is always hope for restoration no matter what the sin. As he says later, "For there is hope for a tree, if it is cut down, that it will sprout again, and that its tender shoots will not cease. Though its root may grow old in the earth, and its stump may die in the ground, yet at the scent of water it will bud and bring forth boughs like a plant" (Job 14:7–9).

If we are to be a faithful friend, a person of restoration, and fulfill the encouragement given in Galatians 6:1 to be a people given to restoration, we will experience some challenging situations with other people. Close lifelong friends may divorce. Others may suffer from addictions. A person we fellowship with could end up in prison. A close associate who reports to you may be caught stealing. The challenging situations are limitless. Will you respond with words of gentleness and restoration? I have always been challenged and humbled by the scripture that follows Galatians 6:1. If we have any doubt about the practical care we're to offer our brothers and sisters in Christ, then consider this: "Bear one another's burdens, and so fulfill the law of Christ" (Gal. 6:2).

This is who you are in Christ: a person who speaks words of restoration and whose words are full of kindness and compassion. You are a new creation, freed from the negative words of this world and the chains of the past. You speak a new language, the language of heaven, thanksgiving, kindness, encouragement, and compassion.

DAILY JOURNAL

1. What is the Lord speaking to me through these verses?

   _____

   _____

   _____

2. Were there any particular words that came out of my mouth today that I need to repent of? I ask the Holy Spirit to touch my heart and keep these words out of my mouth tomorrow.

   _____

   _____

   _____

3. How do I speak words of restoration to those who have stumbled?

   _____

   _____

Epilogue

A Transformed Heart

ONE OF THE most wonderful by-products of my forty-day fast of words was that the person closest to me, my wife, noticed my words change. The Lord was transforming my heart.

My testimony is that I am now a worshipper. Praise is my favorite pastime. Praise is on my lips and fills up my life! I'm not living in the past with my failures and negative experiences. Praising Him leaves me little time for judging others, speaking critical words, being sarcastic, remaining negative, complaining, or gossiping. The cost associated with these negative words is too severe, and I just don't have time for that anymore.

What to do, then, if you have taken the forty-day word fast and find yourself still struggling? There is good news. If you are a tough case like me, then simply repeat the forty days again and again. As you continue in it, you will find your sensitivity to these negative words will grow and your awareness of them in your life will become acute. You will hear your words like you have never heard them in times past. You will become repentant.

If you become serious and desperate about changing the words that come across your lips and need further encouragement, then share with your closest friends or mate what God is doing in you. Tell them the journey you are on. Ask them to pray for you daily that you might remove these destructive words from your mouth. As you know, if we confess our sins to one another He is faithful to forgive us and cleanse us from all of these destructive words (1 John 1:9). The Lord promises too that He has grace for the humble (James 4:6). To reach out and be transparent with others is very humbling.

As a final thought about how to attack these negative words in your life, pray about enlisting the support of a close friend or mate to speak the truth over you when they hear your transgressions with these negative words. Please use caution here and do not broadcast a need for accountability. You don't need to surround yourself with the "word accountability police." You don't need people pointing out what is already true to you—that you stuck your foot in your mouth again with a sarcastic comment. But you could use a mature brother or sister who loves you and will point out the other truth to you—that you are a new creation in Christ and that old things are passed away, all things are new. It is the truth that sets you free. You don't need those negative words anymore. Compassion and kindness are on your lips. You are a person whose speech is being transformed. You don't need someone pointing out your faults; you need someone pointing you up to who you are in Christ.

May the Lord so touch your speech that your testimony will agree with Isaiah: "The Sovereign Lord has given me a well-instructed tongue, to know the word that sustains the weary. He wakens me morning by morning, wakens my ear to listen like one being instructed" (Isa. 50:4, NIV).

NOTES

INTRODUCTION

1. Biblesoft's *New Exhaustive Strong's Numbers and Concordance With Expanded Greek-Hebrew Dictionary*. Copyright © 1994, Biblesoft and International Bible Translators Inc., s.v. *"tsuwm,"* OT 6684.

CHAPTER 1: THE POWER OF WORDS

1. Charles Spurgeon, "Joseph Attacked by the Archers," *Sermons Delivered in Exeter Hall, Strand; by the Rev. C. H. Spurgeon During the Enlargement of New Park Street Chapel, Southwark* (London: Alabaster & Passmore, 1855), 130.

2. Mark Waldman and Andrew Newberg, "The Most Dangerous Word in the World," *Psychology Today*, August 1, 2012, https://www.psychologytoday.com/blog/words-can -change-your-brain/201208/the-most-dangerous-word-in -the-world (accessed April 13, 2015).

3. Julia Layton, "Is It True That If You Do Anything for Three Weeks It Will Become a Habit?", How Stuff Works, http://science.howstuffworks.com/life/inside-the -mind/human-brain/form-a-habit1.htm (accessed April 14, 2015).

4. Catharine Paddock, "Prolonged Fasting 'Re-boots' Immune System," *Medical News Today*, June 6, 2014, .http:// www.medicalnewstoday.com/articles/277860 .php (accessed April 13, 2015).

CHAPTER 3: THE SARCASTIC WOUNDER AND THE CRITIC

1. Merriam-Webster Word Central, s.v. "sarcasm," http:// www.wordcentral.com/cgi-bin/student?sarcasm (accessed April 17, 2015).

2. Merriam-Webster.com, s.v. "criticism," http://www .merriam-webster.com/dictionary/criticism (accessed April 17, 2015).

3. Blue Letter Bible, s.v. "*paraklēsis*," NT: G3874, http://
www.blueletterbible.org/lang/Lexicon/Lexicon
.cfm?Strongs=G3874&t=KJV (accessed April 17, 2015).

CHAPTER 4: LEAVE BEHIND THE
PAST—AND NEGATIVE WORDS

1. Merriam-Webster.com, s.v. "negative," http://www
.merriam-webster.com/dictionary/negative (accessed April 17,
2015).

2. Raychelle Lohmann, "Sibling Bullying," *Psychology
Today*, April 13, 2014, https://www.psychologytoday.com
/blog/teen-angst/201404/sibling-bullying (accessed April 13,
2015).

3. StopBullying.gov, "Facts About Bullying," US Department of Health and Human Services, http://www.stopbullying.
gov/news/media/facts/#listing (accessed April 14, 2015); NoBul-
lying.com, "Bullying Statistics 2014," December 14, 2014,
http://nobullying.com/bullying-statistics-2014/ (accessed April
14, 2015).

CHAPTER 6: THE MOST WICKED OF ALL WORDS

1. Gossip Gawk, www.gossipgawk.com (accessed May 15,
2015).

CHAPTER 7: FIND THE MORE EXCELLENT WAY

1. *Merriam-Webster's Collegiate Dictionary 11th Edition*
(Springfield, MA: Merriam-Webster Inc., 2003), s.v. "optimism."

DAY 6: HEARING AND SPEAKING GOD'S WORDS

1. Norman P. Grubb, *Rees Howells: Intercessor* (Philadel-
phia: Christian Lit. Crusade, 1953), 45.

Day 13: What Comes First?

1. Albert Barnes, "Commentary on Matthew 14:21," Barnes' Notes on the New Testament, "http://www.study light.org/commentaries/bnb/view.cgi?bk=39&ch=14 (accessed April 14, 2015).

Day 14: Behind Enemy Lines

1. Gene Edwards, epigraph to *The Prisoner in the Third Cell* (Wheaton, IL: Tyndale House, 1991).

Day 16: Speech 101

1. Thinkexist.com, "Jalal ad-Din Rumi Quotes," http:// thinkexist.com/quotation/silence-is-the-language-of-god -all-else-is-poor/763267.html (accessed June 30, 2015).

Day 19: Post a Watch

1. Blue Letter Bible, s.v. "*natsar*," http://www.blueletter bible.org/lang/Lexicon/Lexicon.cfm?Strongs=H5341&t=KJV (accessed April 17, 2015).

Day 23: The Taming Work

1. *Cymbeline*, ed. J. M. Nosworthy (London: Cengage Learning, 2007), 3.4.35–40. References are to act, scene, and line.

Day 25: Do Your Words Build?

1. Blue Letter Bible, s.v. "*oikodomē*," http://www.blue letterbible.org/lang/Lexicon/Lexicon.cfm?Strongs=G3619&t =KJV (accessed April 14, 2015).

Day 32: What's Tasty to You?

1. Paul Enck, "Beware the Nocebo Effect," *New York Times,* August 10, 2012, http://www.nytimes.com/2012 /08/12/opinion/sunday/beware-the-nocebo-effect.html? _r=0 (accessed April 14, 2015).

TimCameronPrayer

Advancing Prayer in the Earth

www.timcameronprayer.com